MW00619235

ALGORITHMIC TRADING

Step-By-Step Guide to Develop Your Own Winning
Trading Strategy Using Financial Machine
Learning Without Having to Learn Code

Investors Press

Table of Contents

Introduction

"I have two basic rules about winning in trading as well as in life: 1) If you don't bet, you can't win. 2) If you lose all your chips, you can't bet."

-by Larry Hite

For decades, stock trading was locked behind the door of wealth and exclusivity. When that door opened with the introduction of online trading platforms and discount brokers, a flood of new investors and traders entered the market exchange.

In many ways, the introduction of discount brokers and online trading platforms was a breath of fresh air. It opened up the market and boosted our global economy. It also gave everyone with a bit of cash and an internet connection the opportunity to grow their wealth.

However, when you're just starting out in trading and investment, the world of financial investments can be quite overwhelming, especially if you're starting without much guidance, which is the case with discount brokers.

After all, as a newbie, how do you know what to invest in, how to invest, and when to invest? Well, when embarking on any new venture, the first thing most of us tend to do is jump into some research.

In the time before Google, research often meant pouring over large texts and getting yourself dusty in the library. We're glad to say that those days are long gone.

With increasingly sophisticated technological advancements, trading no longer needs to be a daunting task. These days, there are paper trading accounts and online webinars, all of which are aimed at helping beginners land on their feet.

When you've traversed the financial markets for a bit, you'll be exposed to a plethora of trading techniques, methods, and strategies that you can use when interacting with financial markets. These methods and strategies come in all shapes and sizes and are suited toward every level of expertise there is.

If you're a bit more tech-savvy and are looking to jump into trading and investment, algorithmic trading might be the perfect way to navigate the financial market.

If you're reading this book, chances are pretty high that you've heard about algorithmic trading and are interested in exploring it as a possible avenue of trade and investment.

But, as with all things concerning finance, you know that you should be doing your research before jumping in.

That's where we come in.

This book is aimed at discussing the basics of algorithmic trading and helping you use algo trading as a means of managing your investment portfolio. We're here to answer questions like whether algo trading is better than manual trading and if algo trading even works.

In short, this book is a crash course on algorithmic trading and covers things like the basics of algo trading, its uses, risks and benefits, and how to get started.

It also includes a basic how-to on developing algorithmic strategies, the best practices that you should implement when starting out, and it offers additional resources that you can check out once you've gained all you need to from this book.

Who Is Investors Press? And Why Should You Trust Us?

Now, we know what you're thinking. Who is this author? And what do they know about finance and trading?

And you're absolutely within your rights to ask these questions. Well, we are the team behind Investors Press, a publishing company that specializes in providing resources for traders and investors.

We've studied asset trading and have done extensive research along with experts on the different topics we tackle, and we hope that our experience will help you achieve success in your trading and investing journey. We've done a thorough and exhaustive study on algorithmic trading, and we think that, if you're willing to rise to the challenge, it could be a great tool to add to your arsenal.

We wrote this book to act as a useful resource for beginners and to simplify the complex topic of algorithmic trading. We also intended this book to act as a guide to help beginners navigate the world of trading.

Chapter Overview

Before we jump in, here's a brief overview of what this book offers:

Chapter 1 acts as an introduction to algorithmic trading. This chapter covers the basics of algorithmic trading, how it works, and how it's used by traders and investors.

Chapter 2 discusses what you'll need to know and what you'll need to learn in order to start implementing algorithmic trading. In this chapter, we'll cover the kind of equipment and software you'll need, as well as the skills you'll need to acquire.

Chapter 3 breaks down the steps to start algorithmic trading and covers things like how to develop your own algorithm and trading strategy. It also focuses on helping you test algorithms and strategies.

Chapter 4 presents common trading strategies that are used in algorithmic trading. It also provides tips on how to find trading and arbitrage opportunities.

Chapter 5 focuses on helping you keep your algorithm up-to-date and relevant, which is particularly important given how quickly the market shifts. This chapter also provides tips on how to evaluate your trading strategy in order to maintain efficiency.

Chapter 6 takes a look at risk management and aims to help you identify the risks that come along with algorithmic trading and how to manage them.

Lastly, **Chapter 7** outlines additional resources that you can access if you'd like to further your knowledge on algorithmic trading. In this chapter we've also added the links to these resources if you'd like to jump right in.

Now that you know what you're in for, let's jump in!

Chapter 1:
Basics of Algorithmic Trading

Algorithmic trading is one of the many methods of traversing through financial markets. But, like most trading methods, implementing algorithmic trading and turning it into a viable investment method takes time, patience, and practice.

And, like most trading methods, algorithmic trading requires a unique set of skills. In addition to being well versed in trade and investments, you'll also need to be able to code and program.

But, before we get into the logistics of algorithmic trading, you need to know the basics first.

What is Algorithmic Trading

So, what is algorithmic trading?

In simple terms, algorithmic trading (also known as automated trading) makes use of a computer program that has been given a series of instructions to place a trade. At its core, algorithmic trading is a systematic approach to financial trading.

The computer program, when making use of these instructions (algorithm), can execute trades at a speed and frequency that we humans aren't able to reach. The computer program is based on a mathematical equation, or algorithm, that lays out a defined set of instructions on how the program needs to behave (Seth, 2021).

These instructions include specifics such as which financial instrument to trade, the price points to trade at, and the quantity that should be traded. These algorithms often consist of complex formulas in combination with mathematical models (Chen, 2019). However, while algorithmic trading is automated, it still requires human intervention, particularly given how often financial trends and markets shift.

Due to the automated function which defines algorithmic trading, this method is often used by high volume, high-frequency traders.

Algorithmic trading emerged in the mid-1970s, when the New York Stock Exchange introduced the Designated Order Turnaround (DOT) system. The DOT system involved routing orders from the traders to specialists who were located on the exchange floor (Chen, 2019).

You must remember, in the mid-1970s, the luxury of online trading hadn't yet reared its head, and thus, trade exchanges were often physical locations.

As the years passed and technology improved, electronic trading gained prevalence and, by 2009, over 60% of all trades in the United States were executed electronically (Chen, 2019). These days, electronic trading has become widespread. Discount brokers, and online brokers, are increasingly commonplace.

Algorithmic trading is no exception. There are tons of programmers who write code for algorithmic trading as a means of earning extra income. However, with the prevalence of high-speed internet and fast computers, algorithmic trading is a skill almost anyone can pick up.

With the introduction of artificial intelligence (AI) and machine learning, computer programmers are now able to create algorithms that can improve and update themselves through a process called deep learning. This lessens the need for human intervention and allows the algorithm to adapt to market trends (Chen, 2019).

However, as much as technology has revolutionized financial trade, we would still advise that you keep your eye on your trade and investment profiles when using automated systems such as algorithmic trading.

How Does Algorithmic Trading Work?

As we've mentioned, algorithmic trading is, in essence, a computer program that follows instructions.

For example, let's say you set up a program that has been instructed to:

1. Buy 20 shares of stock once the 50-day moving average exceeds the 200-day moving average.

2. Sell shares whose 50-day moving average shifts below the 200-day moving average.

Now, this is a pretty simple set of instructions, and the computer will trade based on these instructions. The program automatically monitors the stock price of the shares and waits for the moving average of these shares to meet the criteria set out by the instructions before executing a trade.

Now, this might seem overly simplistic, and that's because it is. Algorithmic trading entails much more than just creating a computer program to do all your trading for you. Merely creating a program doesn't mean that it'll be effective at boosting your income.

Algorithmic trading takes work to, well, work.

In order to make algorithmic trading a profitable and viable trading option, you need to do the following:

- Find a trading strategy that works for you and matches your financial goals
- Create an algorithm that suits your trading strategy
- Test your algorithm extensively to make sure that it works as intended
- Create a trading and investment portfolio
- And lastly, monitor and evaluate your algorithm and strategy in order to ensure that it's effective

And that's just the basics!

Now, we're not trying to scare you. While technology has made trading easier, you'll still need to do your due diligence. With something as complex as algorithmic trading, it'll take a lot more than just research.

Before you panic, let's take a breath. This is a beginner's guide, and we'll be helping you through each and every step along the way.

Finding a Trading Strategy

Having an effective trading strategy is the cornerstone of every algorithmic trader. Without a proper strategy, you won't be able to implement an effective algorithm.

The first step when pursuing trade and investment is to find a trading strategy that aligns with your needs and financial goals. The first step toward deciding on a trading strategy is knowing your financial situation and clearly defining your financial goals. You should also consider aspects like how much time you have to spend on trading and the amount of money you want to trade.

Remember, the strategy you choose should be in line with what you'd like to achieve. The entire purpose of a trading strategy is to help you achieve your financial goals.

Now, you have two options here. You could try to develop your own trading strategy or implement one of the many trading strategies that exist within the world of finance. If you're a beginner at trading and trading strategies, we would suggest you check out pre-existing strategies.

However, for interest's sake, let's go over the steps to creating your own strategy. We'll be covering algorithmic trading strategies in Chapter 4.

Creating Your Own Trading Strategy

Before you're able to begin defining your trading strategy, you need to outline a few basic tenets.

Firstly, what financial instrument do you want to trade? Are you focused more on stocks or commodities? Perhaps you'd like to trade futures contracts or options?

The financial instrument you decide to trade will heavily influence your strategy. After all, trading stocks is slightly different than trading options or commodities. If you're a beginner, we would suggest starting with one financial instrument. Once you've become more comfortable and familiar with trading you can branch out and begin diversifying your investment portfolio.

After you've chosen a financial instrument, it's time to come up with a trading idea.

1. **The Idea:** Your trading idea can be anything from wanting to do high volume trades or trading casually. The point is that this idea will form the basis of your strategy (Samuelsson, 2021).

   During this phase, you can be as creative and innovative as you want to be. The only limitation is your own imagination.

   When you come up with your idea, we would suggest browsing trading forums for inspiration.

2. **Backtesting:** Now that you've come up with your trading idea, you need to figure out if it's viable. The easiest way to do this is by 'backtesting' the idea. Basically, this entails testing your newly formed trading strategy on historical data in order to see if the strategy will work or not.

   Backtesting relies heavily on the 'equity curve.' The equity curve is a visual representation of market trends and the variation of the value of trade and investment accounts over a period of time (Burns, 2020). This is generally shown via a graph.

   An upward equity curve means that the trading strategy being used is profitable over time. A downward curve means that your trading strategy doesn't line up with market trends and is unlikely to be profitable.

   Backtesting uses the equity curve to gauge the viability of a trading strategy by focusing on specific buy and sell signals, like the instructions mentioned above.

   While backtesting is a great preliminary test for your trading strategy, we would suggest you take it a step further by employing 'robustness testing.'

3. **Robustness Testing:** More often than not, backtesting isn't enough to ensure the viability of a trading strategy. We like to think about backtesting as a preliminary indicator of

whether you're on the right track in developing a strategy or not.

After all, the only thing that backtesting shows is that your trading strategy is suited to random market babble. It's not a true test of whether your trading strategy will match up to true market trends and behavior.

Robustness testing, also known as stress testing, means putting your trading strategy through various tests, each of which changes certain variables, such as the price data (Bryant, n.d.).

If your trading strategy is 'robust,' it will have relatively muted reactions to the changes in variables, whereas if it's not, it will react disproportionally. In some cases, your trading strategy might fail completely.

The aim here is to give you some idea of how your trading strategy might react in live market conditions. If your trading strategy is unable to handle these changes effectively, chances are, it won't survive in true market conditions.

Conducting stress testing is very important because real-time markets are in a constant state of flux. Robustness testing aims to emulate the constant changes in market trends in order to ensure that the strategy will be able to handle them. It focuses on finding out how your trading strategy will perform once market conditions are no longer ideal (Bryant, n.d.).

4. **Creating Your Portfolio:** Now that you've developed and tested your trading strategy, it's time to create a portfolio of strategies.

It's common practice for experienced traders to have various investment and trade portfolios, each operating on a different trade strategy and often with a different financial instrument.

What makes algorithmic trading so great is that it allows you to run numerous portfolios and strategies at once. Having diversified portfolios running numerous trading strategies is also a great way to protect yourself from risk (Samuelsson, 2021).

This is because if one of the portfolios and strategies fails, you'll have multiple backups and you'll be able to mitigate the loss. Having multiple strategies in place also allows you to adapt easily to market shifts.

While this method of trade is ideal, we wouldn't suggest it to beginners. Having a wide range of portfolios (hopefully a diverse set) can become complicated to manage, especially if you're a beginner and are still finding your feet.

For beginners, we would suggest starting with a single portfolio that follows one trade strategy and focuses on one financial instrument.

5. **Monitoring the Strategies:** Now that your portfolio is all set up, the real fun begins. It's time to monitor the strategy or strategies that you've implemented.

   Now, depending on how much time you have on hand, as well as the intensity of your trade strategy, this could take anywhere from a few minutes to a couple of hours. If you're pressed for time, we would suggest implementing a simple strategy that's easy to keep track of.

   While it can be tempting to leave the algorithm to run your portfolio for you, you should keep in mind that algorithmic trading requires a fair bit of monitoring to ensure that it's working optimally.

   Monitoring your strategy allows you to pick up on any errors in the code or instructions that you might've missed. It also allows you to make sure that your connection hasn't disconnected from the server.

   This strategy is one of the things that will ensure that you're able to mitigate any risks that could come from software or hardware malfunction.

   However, this doesn't mean that you'll have to be glued to your PC for hours at a time. These days, it's possible to check your trading via a remote server. This allows you to check on your portfolio from your cellphone if you find yourself away from home.

How is Algorithmic Trading Used?

Thus far, we've discussed the basics of what algorithmic trading is and how it works, but how is this method used? Well, there are numerous forms of trading that could make use of algorithmic trading.

Remember, algorithmic trading is a systematic approach to active trading and can be used in nearly every form of trade, depending on how it's programmed (Chen, 2019).

In this section, we'll be going over three common trade and investment activities that could use algorithmic trading:

1. **Short-term traders,** market makers, speculators, and sell-side participants often benefit from automated trade executions. With regard to market makers, the addition of algorithmic traders also aids in keeping financial markets sufficiently liquid for buyers and sellers.

   Liquidity within financial markets is especially important because it allows the market to function as intended. That is to say that it allows quick and easy trade and investments.

2. Algorithmic trading is also used by mid-term and long-term investors and buy-side firms. In this case, algorithmic trading is used to buy

large amounts of stocks without influencing market trends and stock prices. This type of algorithmic trading allows traders and investors to make discrete, high-volume trades and investments.

3. More commonly, algorithmic trading is used by systematic traders, who tend to follow market trends. This could include hedge fund traders or pair traders.

   Systematic traders will often prefer to automate their trades according to a set of instructions rather than trading manually, due to the efficiency of automatic trading.

While algorithmic trading is a versatile and effective method of trade and investment, it does not suit every financial market. For example, algorithmic trading works best with financial instruments such as stocks, ETFs, highly liquid futures contracts, and forex pairs.

In essence, algorithmic trading works best in highly liquid financial markets due to the large trading volume and speed associated with automatic trading.

The Advantages and Disadvantages of Algorithmic Trading

There are numerous advantages and disadvantages of algorithmic trading. Before you run full speed ahead with algo trading, it's important that you understand the risks as well as the benefits associated with it.

The Benefits of Algo Trading

Algorithmic trading is often used by large brokerage firms and institutional investors in order to cut down on the costs associated with trading. Studies have shown that algorithmic trading is particularly useful for high-volume traders.

The major benefit of algorithmic trading is that it's often used to increase market liquidity, which allows financial markets to operate as intended.

Additional benefits include:

Speed

By now, you must have realized that a major benefit of algorithmic trading is that it allows for faster and easier trade executions. Due to the trade speed and volume that algorithmic trading allows, it's ideal for scalp trading.

Scalp trading involves profiting from small price fluctuations that occur over a period of time by rapidly buying and selling financial assets at small price increments (Laster, n.d.).

Algorithmic trading also allows you to execute trades based on numerous indicators at speeds that humans often can't reach. This allows you to analyze and execute trades faster, and it provides you with more trading opportunities (Laster, n.d.).

However, while speed is a major benefit to algorithmic trading, it can become an issue if a large number of trades are executed over an extended period of time without human intervention. As mentioned in the previous section, monitoring your trades and trade profile is vitally important to ensure that you don't incur unnecessary losses.

Accuracy

As with everything in finance, accuracy is very important in trading and investments. This is especially true given market trends and fluctuations. Given your level of expertise and experience, you might be able to accurately execute trades at high volumes without much issue.

However, unless you're a professional investor, this level of trade is often inaccessible to the layman trader.

Algorithmic trading often increases the accuracy of trades and reduces mistakes that could arise due to human error (Laster, n.d.). For example, if you're trading manually, you might accidentally buy or sell the wrong asset or buy and sell at the wrong price.

You might also be influenced to make certain trades because of the emotional state you're in. Some days you might feel more reckless and other days you might feel more cautious.

Algorithmic trading eliminates the effects of human emotion and acts only as it has been instructed. It's both predictable and reliable. It's also very effective at mitigating human error.

As discussed in the previous section, algorithmic trading also avoids human error by allowing for backtesting and robustness testing (Laster, n.d.). This allows you to test your algorithm and ensure that it will work the way you intended it to.

By mitigating human error, algorithmic trading also decreases the risks associated with trading manually.

Reduced Costs

As mentioned above, algorithmic trading is often used as a means of reducing the costs associated with trade and investment. Traders won't need to spend hours checking and rechecking markets as trade occurs since trading can be done without your supervision.

This allows you to cut down on costs and reduce the amount of time you'd normally spend trading if you did them manually. This gives you the freedom to spend your time as you choose, without being chained to your PC.

The Disadvantages of Algorithmic Trading

While algorithmic trading comes with numerous advantages, it also carries its fair share of disadvantages and risks. It's important to understand the disadvantages associated with algorithmic trading before jumping in.

Technical Errors

One of the biggest disadvantages of algorithmic trading is experiencing technical errors. After all, algorithmic trading is dependent on running specific software, having access to certain hardware, and being able to program the algorithm effectively.

Issues such as power failures, disconnecting servers, and software and hardware crashes are all risks associated with algorithmic trading.

If a power failure occurs or you lose your internet connection, trades will fail to be sent to the market and will go unexecuted; this could lead to losses.

There could also be a misalignment between projected trades generated by the algorithm and the actual trades executed if your hardware or software isn't up to standard.

Algorithmic trading is extremely technical, and there will be a steep learning curve when you're starting out. In addition to the skills you'll need to pick up, algorithmic trading also requires certain equipment, hardware, and software in order to operate. We discuss the hardware and software requirements of algorithmic trading in Chapter 2.

Over-Optimization

With algorithmic trading, you run the risk of developing a trading strategy that looks great on paper but ultimately fails in real-time market exchanges. What we mean by this is that your trading strategy might work well when backtesting but could still fail when introduced to real-time markets.

This is known as over-optimization. If your trading strategy is over-optimized, it'll exhibit excessive curve-fitting that excels in back-testing but is unable to keep up in live trading.

A good way to avoid over-optimization is to subject your trading strategy to numerous stress tests in order to see how it might behave when subjected to live trading. Even then, we would suggest trying your trading strategy with paper trading accounts in order to see if it'll be able to stand up against real-time market trends.

Paper trading accounts are a great resource for testing new trading strategies in simulated market exchanges. They're commonly offered by discount and online brokers.

Should You Shift From Manual Trading to Algorithmic Trading?

In general, there are two basic ways that you can interact with financial market exchanges. The first, which we have been discussing, is algorithmic or automated trading.

As we've discussed, automated trading is dependent on an algorithm and certain software. It requires very little human intervention and runs as the algorithm intends.

The second way is via manual trading. Manual trading is the more 'traditional' means of trading and has been around since the emergence of financial trade and investments. Manual trading, as the name implies, means trading as you want without the intervention of an algorithm. You decide when, where, and how to trade.

Every decision made comes from you.

Before we get into whether you should forgo manual trading for algo trading, let's take a look at the ins and outs of manual trading and all that it entails.

Manual Trading

Manual trading is, in essence, hands-on trading. You, as the trader, will personally execute trades and investments. This often means having to read market trends and price point fluctuations to see if they match your strategy and then deciding whether or not to execute a trade.

If you've decided to go through with the trade, you'll have to do it manually.

Nothing is automated.

Manual trading means that most of the work is done by the trader. Therefore, your output will only be as good as your input. How much profit you make will be determined by how many successful trades you're able to execute, as well as how quickly you're able to execute them, and how much time you have to spend dedicated to trading and investment.

Benefits to Manual Trading

Here are a few benefits to manual trading:

- Manual trading helps traders and investors adapt to and learn more about the financial market that they're interacting with. It also helps you familiarize yourself with the tools, graphs, and methods used when making trades. For example, these are technical and fundamental analysis tools.

If you're a beginner in trading, manual trading is a great way to wrap your head around the ins and outs of trading and all the variables that influence market prices and fluctuations.

If you're looking to build your knowledge, manual trading is the way to go.

- Manual trading gives you absolute control over your trades and investments. It also allows you full control of your portfolio management. This is great if you're working in live market exchanges because you make all the decisions.

You decide where and how to spend your money when trading and investing.

- Manual trading also allows you to quickly figure out whether a trading strategy is working for you and identify little variables that need tweaking in order to improve your strategy.

You're also able to quickly identify weaknesses and mistakes in your trading strategy since you'll be working with it hands-on.

This allows you to quickly alter your trading strategy and mitigate preventable losses.

Drawbacks to Manual Trading

Here are a few common drawbacks to using manual trading:

- The biggest drawback to manual trading is that it takes time. You'll need to do your own research, place your orders and trades based on this research, read market trends, keep track of financial news, and spend a good deal of time reviewing your trade strategies to assess their efficiency and profitability.

  This takes time and an extensive amount of effort and energy. While a few of these steps can be automated, and most online brokers have streamlined their platforms to make this easier, it'll still require you to carve out time in your day to focus on your portfolio.

- Manual trading requires a lot of discipline and self-restraint in order to be successful. This means that you can't let your emotions influence your trading and investments.

  Oftentimes, you might feel compelled to execute certain trades because you're scared of missing out on 'the next big thing' or because you feel pressured by other traders. This could cause you to begin 'gambling' with your trades instead of executing them according to a sound strategy.

  This opens you up to unnecessary risks and losses.

- Manual trading also comes with the disadvantage of falling prey to human error. We're all human, and thus we're prone to making mistakes. Trading is no exception. You could sell the wrong asset or invest in the wrong stock with a simple tap of a button.

This could cause you unnecessary losses.

Knowing that you caused yourself a loss can also be difficult to come to terms with. In fact, many traders struggle with being solely accountable for their portfolios.

Manual Trading vs. Algorithmic Trading

So, which method should you go with? Manual trading or algorithmic trading?

Well, the answer to that question is kind of complicated.

Firstly, we'd like to ask you what you wish to achieve with trading and investment, what your financial goals are, and why you would want to trade and invest.

If you can answer these, the next question becomes how involved you would like to be: would you prefer a hands-on approach, or would you prefer a more relaxed approach?

How much time do you have?

The method you choose needs to suit your needs, wants, and lifestyle. It would be easy for us to sit here and say *go with manual trading!* Or *go with automated trading!* But the truth is, the decision lies with you.

If you're reading this book, the chances are that you've already made your decision and have chosen to go with algorithmic trading. This means that you want a bit more freedom, a little less control, and a more systematic approach when it comes to trade.

That being said, just because you go with algorithmic trading now doesn't mean that manual trading is closed to you. If you have the time and energy, you could have it all.

Chapter 2:
Algorithmic Trading
Requirements

In the days of the old, trades and investments were reserved for the elite of society; but with the introduction of online and discount brokers, this has changed.

Now, anyone with a cell phone and internet connection can access financial markets for trades and investments. Beginners will still need to learn a few valuable skills; like being able to read market trends, make market predictions, and test out various trade methods in order to make successful trades, but it's all within reach.

However, unlike most trading and investing methods, algorithmic trading requires a bit more than just an internet connection and basic trading knowledge. If you want to be proficient in algorithmic trading and make it a viable trading option, you'll need to know how to program your algorithm and the hardware and software to run the algorithm.

This chapter discusses what you'll need to know and learn in order to start algorithmic trading. It also goes into the equipment you'll need (yes, algorithmic training requires specific hardware) and the software requirements.

The first section of this chapter covers the technical requirements (hardware) of algorithmic trading. The second focuses on the software you'll need to operate the algorithm, and the third focuses on identifying trading platforms that are ideal for algorithmic trading.

The last few sections of this chapter focus on the knowledge and skills you'll need to acquire, such as programming and the basics of trade, as well as a few tips on programming for beginners.

By the end of this chapter, you should have some idea of what you'll need to get started in algorithmic trading.

Hardware Requirements

Given that algorithm trading is made possible by using a computer program, one of the main hardware components you'll need is a computer. Now, if you think that your laptop will cut it, you're wrong.

Most mainstream and even gaming laptops won't be able to handle the pressure of running the program, software, and making trades without running the risk of overheating and crashing.

Instead, if you're looking to get into algorithmic trading, we suggest you invest in a 'trading computer.' Regardless of whether you're into day trading, swing trading, or algorithmic trading, a trading computer is a must.

Now, a 'trading computer' isn't some magical machine that'll turn you into a trading genius. It's a simple mid-range desktop computer that can be able to handle the software and programs you need to run without overheating or crashing and is used primarily for trading.

While a trading computer isn't much different from a normal computer, there are a few spec-specific features you need be focused on if you plan to build or buy a trading PC:

The CPU

The first thing you should be focusing on when buying or building a trading PC is the CPU. The CPU is the central processing unit and is present in nearly every electronic device, such as computers, cell phones, smart watches, e-readers, and even your thermostat. The CPU is in charge of processing and executing all instructions given to it. In many ways, it acts as the brain of the device.

Therefore, the faster the CPU is able to process and execute instructions, the faster your PC will be able to run. This will increase the speed at which the algorithm will be able to execute trades (Samuelsson, 2019).

With algorithmic trading, the difference between a fast and slow CPU is quite stark, and having a slow CPU could cost you. Having a fast CP also speeds up the trading process and frees up more time for research and strategy development (Samuelsson, 2019).

Now, when choosing a CPU, there's one key thing you should consider, and that's whether to go for a single core or multicore CPU.

Simply put: a single-core processor has one core, while multicore processors have numerous small processors that have been packed into a single chip.

In theory, multicore CPUs are much faster than single-core CPUs. Since their introduction in 2001, multicore CPUs have gained mass popularity, and these days most mainstream computers come with 16-32 cores.

However, multicore CPUs are not without their limitations. More often than not, trading platforms struggle to use all cores effectively (Samuelsson, 2019). Some trading platforms are better at handling multicore processors, and there's been a shift toward platforms increasing their support capabilities.

Given the rapid improvements in technology, we would suggest you go for a multicore CPU. The chances are that most trading platforms will update their software in order to keep up with the times.

The Graphics Card

For most PC users, purchasing a fancy graphics card isn't something that they think about. When many start out in trading, getting a trading PC and a high-end graphics card never crossed their minds. Many assume it was something only high-end gamers needed.

How far from the truth that was.

These days, graphics cards are not only used by gamers and video editors, but also by crypto traders in order to mine cryptocurrency, and you guessed it, algorithmic traders.

The graphics card is essentially an expansion card that's responsible for rendering an image onto your monitor. Therefore, the better the graphics card, the better and smoother the image will be.

A great graphics card will help a trading computer run more smoothly and help you keep track of numerous graphs, charts, and tables when doing research on a specific financial instrument or when trying to read market trends.

In most cases, I'd recommend you invest in two monitors since it makes keeping track of news feeds and market trends much easier. Having a great graphics card makes this much easier and gives you a crisp display (Solanki, 2020).

RAM

RAM, random access memory, is a key component of any PC system. RAM stores the information that's actively being used by the computer so that it can be easily and quickly accessed. RAM is short-term memory.

In essence, the speed and performance of your PC are directly related to how much RAM you have installed. The more RAM you have, the faster and more efficient your PC will be.

Having enough RAM is critical when building or buying a trading computer to ensure that it's able to function properly (Samuelsson, 2019). The amount of

RAM you'll need will depend on how spec-intensive the software and apps you'll be using will be.

As a general rule of thumb, a basic trading computer needs around 8GB of RAM; however, we would recommend that you aim a bit higher, for around 16 to 32GB.

The Hard Drive

The hard drive, also known as the hard disk drive, is an internally installed component that stores all your videos, documents, applications, your operating system, and pictures. In many ways, the hard drive can be thought of as a storage box. It holds pretty much everything.

Having a large hard drive isn't considered particularly important when building a trading PC. While the hard drive's main purpose is to act as a storage vault, it also has a huge impact on how quickly your PC boots up and how quickly applications and software are able to load.

Because of this, having a good hard drive is something you should seriously consider when purchasing or building a trading computer.

There are two kinds of hard drives. The first is the general HDD (hard disk drive) which nearly every computer comes equipped with. The second is the fancier SSD (solid-state drive).

When investing in a trading PC, we would recommend you go for an SSD drive instead of the more common HDD drive. This is because the SSD drive has been proven to be much faster than the HDD and will cut your boot and loading times in half.

However, SSD drives are a bit pricier than HDD drives, and if you're unable to afford it, we would suggest going with a really good HDD. It'll serve the same purpose but might be a bit slower.

Cooling

Given that a trading PC often runs at maximum capacity for extended periods of time, having an effective cooling system in place is essential to prevent overheating.

Running at max capacity for a long time will cause your PC to generate large amounts of heat and, in order to avoid overheating, the PC will forcibly slow down (Samuelsson, 2021).

To prevent this from happening, most PCs come fitted with air coolers. However, depending on the quality of the PC, these air coolers can be incredibly noisy when performing at max capacity and usually aren't able to cool the PC down enough to be very effective.

We would advise that you upgrade your cooling system by either adding better fans or installing liquid coolers. Liquid coolers are much more efficient than air coolers and are much quieter as well. However, keep in mind that liquid coolers are also much more expensive than air coolers.

The Internet Connection

Having a great, fast, and secure internet connection is essential to any kind of trade. Your internet connection is your link to financial markets and your broker platform. It is, in essence, your gateway to trades and investments.

If you want to ensure that your algorithm operates the way it should, you need a reliable internet connection.

We would recommend that you invest in some kind of backup just in case your internet fails. This could be an extra modem or even your smartphone hotspot. While not the most elegant solution, being able to connect your PC to your smartphone's hotspot can help you close any open positions and prevent you from incurring unnecessary losses.

The Minimum and Recommended Specifications for a Trading PC

Minimum Requirements		Recommended Requirements	
CPU	CPU with 4 cores	CPU	CPU with 8 cores
RAM	8GB	RAM	16GB
Storage	240GB SSD	Storage	240GB SSD

Software Requirements

Much like with the hardware requirements, you have the option of either building or programming or buying the software you'll need for algorithmic trading.

Buying ready-made software is quick and easy. However, they're not without their downsides. While buying your trading software might save you time, they won't save you money. Algorithmic software is often incredibly costly, and it might also be filled with flaws that, if ignored, could lead to unnecessary losses (Seth, 2021b).

The high costs of the software might also cut into the viability of your algorithm trading, so that's something to keep in mind.

On the other hand, building your own software allows you to customize it to your needs and offers you great flexibility (Seth, 2021b). It also doesn't cost nearly as much as buying software. However, building your own software will require time, tremendous effort, and deep knowledge of programming and how financial markets and trading work.

Key Components Every Algorithmic Trading Software Should Have

No matter if you decide to buy or build, there are a few key components that every algorithmic trading software needs in order to be viable.

Connectivity to Various Financial Markets

The most important component to any trading software is that it should have access to and be able to connect to various financial markets. This should be at both a national and international scope.

As a trader, you'll be working across multiple market exchanges. Each market will grant you access to various data feeds, and these data feeds are likely to differ in format. The software you buy or build will need to be able to accept feeds in different formats (Seth, 2021b).

If this proves too much of a challenge, you could try going with third-party data vendors, such as Reuters and Bloomberg. These data vendors provide you with aggregate market data obtained from various market exchanges. The data is also offered in a single, uniform format.

The key here is to make sure that your software should be able to process this data as required.

Backtesting with Historical Data

Another key feature that every trading software should have is the ability to conduct backtesting simulations on historical data sets. As previously discussed, backtesting involves imposing a trading strategy on historical data in order to simulate live trade, done with the aim of testing out a trading strategy in order to gauge its viability in live trading.

Backtesting is a mandatory feature; don't overlook its importance and value.

The Availability of Company and Market Data

Trading software also needs to have easy access to real-time market data feeds and company feeds. This function should be built into the system, and it should be able to easily integrate and process this information from various sources (Seth, 2021b).

Real-time data feeds contain important information like company fundamentals, company earnings, and P/E ratios. This information is essential for any trader and investor.

Latency

Latency is a time-delayed response to the movement of data points from one application to another (Seth, 2021b). For example, it might take 0.3 seconds for a price quote to register from one exchange to your software's data center (DC), it might then take 0.2 for the information to travel from your data center to your screen, and 0.3 seconds for your software to process the information.

It could then take another 0.2 seconds for your algorithm to analyze this information and place a trade, 0.4 seconds for the trade to reach the broker, and 0.3 seconds for the trade to be executed.

Given how quickly price point movements occur on the market exchange, it is likely that, within the few seconds it takes to execute a trade, the price of that asset would've changed multiple times.

In order to avoid delay and trade on the price point you want, it's important to keep the latency time as low as possible and, ideally, reduce it to microseconds. You can do this by having a direct connection to the exchange, which eliminates the need for a vendor (the middle man).

Programming that is Independent of the Platform

While it's not a requirement, having programming that's independent of the platform and software you're using is a good idea for long-term planning.

Generally, programming languages have dedicated platforms that work specifically for that software or platform. Whether you decide to build or buy, it's advised that you choose a programming language that differs from the one used by the platform you're going with.

The idea here is to prepare for any future changes that your trading strategy and algorithm might take.

Customization

Another important component of trading software is being able to customize it to suit your needs and trading strategy.

If you choose to buy, most algorithmic trading software comes with built-in algorithms. This potentially saves you time and effort; however, you should be able to completely customize the parameters of the algorithm to fit your own trade strategy.

If you buy the wrong software, you might find yourself being constrained by fixed functionality that you're unable to change.

In addition to this, being able to write your own custom programs within the software is another key feature you need to look for. This allows you to further customize and experiment with various strategies and trading concepts (Seth, 2021b).

Ideally, you should go with trading software that allows you to use your preferred programming language.

Choosing a Trading Platform

Now that you have your software and algorithm ready and hopefully tested, it's time to decide on a trading platform. But what is a trading platform? Why do you need it?

In simple terms, a trading platform is an online website or application where traders and investors are able to conduct trade and investments. Numerous online and discount brokers offer their own trading platforms either for free or at low rates, depending on the account type you hold and the broker you've chosen.

Generally, trading platforms also offer a plethora of additional services such as real-time data feeds, charting software, and premium analysis (*Trading Platform*, 2021). These services are aimed at making trade and investment as easy and as effective as possible.

There are two kinds of trading platforms: the first and most common are commercial websites, and the second are prop platforms. Commercial websites are aimed toward investors and day traders (*Trading Platform*, 2021). These kinds of trading platforms are generally easy to use and come with a vast selection of features such as educational resources, research data, news feeds, and maps.

On the other hand, prop platforms are customizable platforms developed by large brokers specifically to match their needs, style of trading, and demands.

Currently, there are hundreds of trading platforms, and deciding on which one to go with can get quite overwhelming, especially for beginners. As a general rule of thumb, you should choose a trading platform based on your trading style, trading strategy, and your financial and trading goals. You should also choose a trading platform that works well with an algorithmic trading method.

Here are a few additional factors that you should consider when choosing a trading platform:

Asset Classes

Before choosing a trading platform, you should ensure that the platform you're going for offers the asset classes that you've decided to trade. This could be stocks, bonds, etc.

Therefore, if you want to trade stocks, don't go for a platform that only supports equities. Most trading platforms support more than one asset class, which is great. Often, online brokers will offer special perks and discounts for certain asset classes. We would advise that you go for a trading platform that not only supports the asset classes of your choice but also offers perks and discounts for your chosen asset classes.

Data

As with everything in trading and investing, having access to up-to-date, relevant data is essential. The trading platform you choose should offer access to extensive, high-quality data. Some trading platforms might charge a fee for access to this information.

Ideally, you'll be able to find a trading platform that offers access to their data for free.

Broker Integration

Being able to link your algorithm to a trading platform is essential to algorithmic trading.

Unfortunately, not all algorithmic trading platforms will let you trade through them. It generally depends on whether or not the trading platform provider is a broker. If the platform provider isn't a broker, the chances are that they will allow broker integration and allow you to link your algorithm to the platform.

There are also a few platforms that don't offer any live trading support at all; this means that you won't be able to trade through them. With these kinds of platforms, all you can use them for is research and development.

It goes without saying that you should go for a trading platform that supports broker integration and allows you to link your algorithm to the platform.

Intellectual Property

A key concern for any algorithmic trader is being able to maintain the intellectual property (ownership) of the algorithms they've developed. Therefore, it's very important to find a trading platform that doesn't claim ownership rights to your algorithm if it's developed on their platform.

If this is something you're especially concerned about, we would advise you to go with a platform that lets you develop your algorithm on your own computer and then link it to the platform. This is by far the safest way to maintain your ownership rights.

Competitions and Licensing

These days, most platforms host competitions quite regularly. In these competitions, you can submit your algorithm (if it meets specific requirements) and battle it out against a ton of other algorithms (Louis, 2020).

If your algorithm wins, you could get all kinds of fun prizes or cash rewards.

Trading platforms could also offer algorithm traders the opportunity to license their algorithms and have them become officially recognized algorithms.

While these perks aren't necessarily essential to the viability and success of your algorithm trading venture, they are nice additions.

Programming Languages

Ensuring that the programming language of the trading platform supports the language you've used to develop your algorithm is essential if you want to be able to link your algorithm to the platform (Louis, 2020).

Even so, you'll still be required to learn the platform's API if you want to develop your algorithm on their platform. However, this shouldn't be much of an issue if you choose a platform that allows you to develop an algorithm on your own computer instead of on the platform.

The Knowledge Requirements

As you might have gathered by now, algorithmic trading requires more than just a fancy trading computer and access to a great trading platform. If you want to be a successful algorithmic trader, there are quite a few skills you'll need to pick up.

The first skill you'll need to learn is the **basics of trading**. This includes things like being able to read market trends, knowing what a stop order is, knowing what a limit order is, and understanding margin requirements.

There's much more to trading than just that. You'll need to know when to execute trades, when to buy and sell, and how to make the market work for you.

With the increasing popularity of trading and investing, there are numerous resources available. Many trading brokers also offer educational resources such as webinars, tutorials, and paper-trading accounts that are ideal for beginners.

If you're anything like us, you learn best by doing, and so we'd recommend you go for a paper trading account.

We'd also recommend you read more books on trading, like this one, especially those focused on the aspects of trade that interest you most. There are also numerous videos on trading and investing that you could check out online.

The key takeaway here is to learn as much as you can before moving on to live trading.

A second important skill, and something you probably weren't expecting, is **math**. Yes, we said it, if you want to be good at algorithmic trading, you need to be good at math. This entails having a good understanding of financial calculations, basic statistics, and computer trading performance metrics (Davey, 2019).

You'll also want to have a working knowledge of Microsoft Excel or some other data manipulation program such as MatLab. These programs are quite useful when supplementing your trading strategy analysis.

As much as it pains us to say, the better you are at math, the better you'll be as an algorithmic trader.

The last skill you'll need to succeed in algorithmic trading is **knowing how to run the trading platform you've chosen**. Now, this skill isn't too hard to learn. All it takes is fiddling around with the platform a little and getting used to the mechanisms.

The best way to get acquainted with a trading platform is to open a paper trading account. This allows you to try out the platform and get used to it without committing. Closely related to this skill is being able to **follow an established scientific approach** and **learning how to develop a trading system**.

Being able to develop a sound trading system is important for designing and testing your algorithmic strategies (Davey, 2019).

The last, and probably most important skill that you'll need to learn, is **programming**. A key part of developing your own algorithm is knowing how to program and knowing which programming language will best suit your needs.

Knowing how to program is also valuable when choosing a trading software since it'll help you understand how the different software operate and which will work best for you. In addition to this, you might want to learn various programming languages as well because different platforms require different programming abilities.

The key here is to do your research and become proficient in whatever programming language is required by the trading platform (Davey, 2019).

Tips for Beginners in Programming

Approaching programming as a newbie can be quite scary. There are so many programming languages around that it can feel overwhelming. But, if you stick with it, programming can be incredibly fun and stimulating.

It's a skill that has thousands of applications. You can use your skill to create algorithms, video games, and new software. The possibilities are truly endless.

But let's reel it in a bit. In this section, I'll be giving you a few tips on how to start in programming as a beginner, with a specific focus on finance and algorithmic trading.

Google is Your Friend

Our first tip is don't be afraid to use Google. As a newbie programmer, chances are you'll make mistakes, stumble around, and get stuck trying to make codes work. If you ever feel stuck and helpless, ask Google.

There are tons of helpful videos and programming forums online; it's just a simple search away. Programming forums and tutorials are fantastic resources that you can use to improve both your skill and confidence with programming.

If you're struggling with certain commands, Google the solution. There's nothing wrong with finding answers instead of struggling your way through it. Don't be afraid to use the resources available to you.

And besides, Google is completely free, so you might as well use it.

Give it Time

This might go without saying, but give yourself time. Programming is a difficult skill to pick up, and you won't become an expert overnight. We recommend that you give yourself the time and space to fail and learn.

Think of it as a marathon rather than a sprint.

The key takeaway here is to jump in and just start. Half the battle is showing up.

Explore as Much as You Can

As we've said, programming can be intimidating. When starting out, you might try to stick to the rules and conventions as much as possible. Now, this isn't a bad thing. Following conventions is how you familiarize yourself with a new craft.

However, don't be afraid to think for yourself and try new things.

If there's a specific coding task you'd like to complete, think about how you'd like to do it. What are the steps you'd like to follow when coding? Think about the steps that are required and how you'd like to do them.

This allows you to use your creativity, and who knows, you might come up with new and exciting ways to solve problems.

Don't be Afraid to use the Print Command in R

If you're feeling intimidated by long strings of complex code and find yourself stuck on figuring out how the code works and what it does, don't be afraid to use the print command.

By simply copying the code in R, you can use the print command to help you understand how the code works and what its key functions are.

You can also use the Ctrl+Enter combination to see the code line-by-line and see the results of the console.

Chapter 3:
Getting Started with Algorithmic Trading

So, you've picked up the skills you need, you've bought or built a trading computer, and you've developed your own algorithm. What comes next?

At this point in your journey, we would assume that you've backtested and stress-tested your algorithm, and you've decided on your trading software and trading platforms. You're ready and jump in and get going.

It's all systems go!

We hate to be the party pooper, but, at this point, we would urge you to slow down.

Caution: slow down and really think about what the next couple of steps are going to look like.

In this chapter, we'll be discussing the steps you'll need to take to start algorithmic trading. We'll be taking a deep dive into how to develop your own algorithm, and we'll be providing an example of an algorithm used for trading.

But before we get to that, we'll also be going over the important things you'll need to consider before jumping in.

In many ways, this little pitstop is the point of no return. After this, you'll be fully immersed in the world of trading, and you wouldn't want all your hard work and efforts to go to waste.

Key Considerations Before Starting

Right now, you're standing on the precipice of change. Depending on where your head's at, this might be the moment before you become a fully-fledged trader, or it could be the moment you decide that this just isn't for you.

You might decide to plunge forward or turn around.

However, before you make that decision, here are a few things you should consider.

Algo Trading is Time-Consuming

Algorithmic trading is, by nature, automated trading, and this might leave you with the impression that you won't have to do much besides setting up the PC, let the algorithm run, and then rake in cash.

Unfortunately, this is hardly the case.

While the algorithm is able to run on its own, it needs human intervention and monitoring. You'll need to take time to reevaluate and reprogram your algorithm to suit shifting market trends.

You'll also need to closely monitor your algorithm to ensure that it's functioning the way you intended it to and that there aren't any flaws or oversights that could cause unnecessary loss.

You'll also need to adjust your algorithm if you decide to try out a different trading strategy.

Trading Requires Capital

Trades and investments require capital, and algorithmic trading is no different. If you want to start trading and investing, you're going to need money.

The amount you'll need to get started will vary depending on the financial market and financial instrument you choose. If you're aiming to day trade stocks, you'll need at least $25,000. Trading Forex and Futures might require less capital.

There are also costs involved with opening an account with an online or discount broker. With brokers, there are often account minimums, commission fees, and transaction fees attached to the services they provide. The trading costs will vary from broker to broker. We would advise that you carefully check out the fees structure of the broker you choose in order to avoid incurring hidden fees.

You'll probably also spend a considerable amount on purchasing or buying a trading PC and getting a hold of the various software that you'll need in order to begin algorithmic trading.

Finally, depending on whether you're a programmer or a complete newbie, you might also spend money on coding and programming courses in order to build your skill.

Goals and Objectives

Before you begin, you need to have firm, clear answers to three questions:

1. What are your financial goals?
2. What financial asset do you want to trade?
3. How much time can you commit to trading?

The key here is to have solid goals and objectives that will help you create your algorithm and decide on a solid trading strategy. Remember, you want your algorithm to work for you and help you achieve your goals.

Knowing exactly what you want and how you want to trade also helps you create your algorithm. After all, the algorithm is merely a set of instructions on how to trade. In order to code those instructions, you need to have a clear idea of your trading strategy and how to implement it.

Developing a Trading Algorithm

Developing a trading algorithm is nothing to scoff at, as you can probably tell from the long list of requirements we mentioned in Chapter 2.

An effective trading algorithm must be able to identify trade (buy and sell) opportunities and be able to execute trades according to a predetermined trading strategy. The trick is being able to convert your chosen trading strategy into lines of code that will form the trading algorithm. This algorithm will also need to be programmed to be able to access trading accounts in order to execute trades effectively.

So, how do you start?

Developing an Effective Strategy

Now, we know we've mentioned this before, and you're probably a bit sick of hearing it, but it bears repeating.

You need an effective trading strategy and, while you might have one, have you thought about how easy your trading strategy would be to code?

As a general rule of thumb, the more subjective and complex your trading strategy is, the harder it'll be to code. On the other hand, the more rule-based, structured, and simple your trading strategy is, the easier it'll be to code (Mitchell, 2021).

In general, rule-based strategies are much easier to code because they're often structured around simple instructions such as stop losses and price targets that are based on quantifiable data or price point movements (Mitchell, 2021).

These kinds of strategies are also easily copied and tested. If you're not totally comfortable coming up with your own trading strategy, there are many available online.

A resource that you could explore is Quantapedia. This website gives you access to a plethora of academic papers on trading and trading results for numerous quantitative trading methods.

No matter what your skill level is in both trading and

programming, we would recommend that you go with a rule-based trading strategy. Algorithmic trading is complicated enough as it is without making things harder by trying to code a complex trading strategy.

After all, coding takes time, and it needs to be tested and retested multiple times in order to work out all the kinks and bugs. Choosing a rule-based strategy will just aid in making your experience easier. In our knowledge and experience, the simpler the strategy, the more effective it is.

Characteristics of a Sound Trading Strategy

When choosing a trading strategy, it's important to be sure about what you would want it to accomplish. Often, it's easier to go for the easiest solution, and while that isn't necessarily a bad idea, we would recommend you do a bit more research.

Read trading blogs and forums. Check out academic finance journals and trading magazines. Basically, explore the world of trading and finance as much as you can.

Your preliminary research should be based on your personal characteristics, such as your risk profile, the amount of time you'll be able to commit, and the amount of capital you're able to set aside for trades.

That being said, here are a few key characteristics that every effective trading strategy should be:

1. Prudent of market changes
2. Based on reputable statistical methods
3. Rule-based

It should also have:

1. Clearly defined rules on when to enter, when to exit, and when to execute a trade.

2. Great portfolio management

3. Risk management

4. Make provisions for the unexpected

Figure Out What Information Your Algorithm Should Capture:

The next step is to clearly define what information your algorithm needs to capture and identify. Now, this shouldn't be too hard to figure out since it should be a key part of your trading strategy.

The aim here is to help your algorithm take advantage of market trends and behaviors (Johnston, 2021). In addition to this, we would also advise against building your strategy around one-time market inefficiencies because market inefficiencies are unidentifiable. There really would be no way of knowing whether the success or failure of your strategy happened by accident.

Now, depending on the trading strategy you choose, there are various methods that take advantage of certain market trends and behaviors. Strategies can take advantage of:

- Macroeconomic news such as interest rate changes

- Fundamental analysis such as revenue data or earnings release notes

- Technical analysis information like moving averages
- Microstructure news like trade infrastructure
- Statistical analysis such as co-integration

Now, these sources of information each contain various technical indicators that you could use in your trading algorithm. Once you become proficient at coding and trading, you could have your algorithm focus on a combination of indicators, depending on how much your trading strategy evolves.

A few popular technical indicators include:

- Moving averages
- Stochastics
- Relative strength index
- Parabolic SAR
- Relative vigor index

Once your algorithm is able to effectively and accurately capture information and process it, it'll be able to use this information (in combination with the instructions) to buy and sell financial assets and successfully execute trades.

The technical indicators mentioned are important for setting rules because, depending on their values, they'll be the trigger for your algorithm to buy or sell an asset.

You'll also need to get benchmarks to compare your strategy against!

Translate Your Trading Strategy into Code

Here's where the real fun (and the real headache) starts!

As we've mentioned before, before you're able to turn your strategy into code, there are a few key skills you'll need to pick up. Thus far, we've discussed understanding the basics of programming and having a working knowledge of trading and financial market exchanges.

In addition to this, you'll need to understand technical, fundamental, and sentimental analysis, and the inputs, variables, and math features that come along with coding.

Technical, Fundamental, and Sentimental Analysis

Having a good understanding of technical, fundamental, and sentimental analysis will help you create your code because you'll be able to understand how the indicators mentioned above work and what they mean.

But, what is technical, fundamental, and sentimental analysis?

Well, **technical analysis** is the belief that past market trends and behaviors have a direct influence over future market trends, movements, and behaviors (*Fundamental, Technical and Sentiment Analysis*, 2018).

Technical analysis traders thus rely heavily on historical data such as trend and chart analysis in order to predict potential price fluctuations and market trends. These charts generally represent price point movements over a certain period of time. By reading and analyzing these charts, traders aim to figure out future supply and demand trends of specific financial assets.

Key indicators for whether to buy or sell are the support and resistance levels. Other indicators include oscillators, trends, and volume indicators. These help traders figure out price trends.

Sentimental Analysis is more short-term than technical analysis and is focused on the sentiments (actions) of traders in general. For example, a technical analyst might predict that a financial asset is going to experience upward growth. However, the asset might remain down due to the mood of the traders.

This means that a large majority of traders have chosen a down position for some unknown reason.

These trader sentiments can be used to help traders take a particular position. Traders that follow sentimental analysis are also known as contrarians because they often invest against the trend. This is done with the belief that the market always tends to go against sentiments.

Fundamental analysis is all about studying the factors that could have an effect on the price of a financial asset. This kind of analysis is heavily dependent on the central bank of each country and the expected interest rates that they release.

It's believed that interest rate hikes can increase the value of an asset long-term. Additional factors that fundamental analysts focus on are the GDP, inflation rates, NFP releases, and population growth. Therefore, keeping up with current news is vital to a fundamental trader.

This kind of analysis is generally used in forex and commodity trading.

When creating an algorithm, understanding these analyses are vital to be able to use the technical indicators above.

Inputs, Variables, and Mathematics Features

Much like the fundamental, technical, and sentimental analyzes mentioned above, inputs, variables, and mathematical features are important when developing an algorithm.

Inputs are generally assigned to other 'nodes' in order to create an algorithm. There are four kinds of inputs that you should be aware of:

- String
- Integer
- Boolean
- Number

The **variables** generally correspond to each data type. There are four data types that you should concern yourself with:

1. Boolean

2. Text

3. Number

4. Date time

Variables are important because they'll tell your algorithm what to do and when to do it.

The **mathematical features** are pretty straightforward. These are the =, +, and - signs, to name a few.

The final aspect you should focus on is **logic,** and we don't mean common sense. Logic includes **AND**, and **Or**. For example, the algorithm could be directed to open a buy trade when the Stochastics is at 28 AND/OR when the RSI value is 30. In this case, you can use both.

In simple terms, the logic function can be used when instructing the algorithm on when to enter and exit positions.

Coding an Algorithmic Trading Strategy

Converting your trading strategy into code is where the fun begins. In our experience, this was where we were able to be the most creative. Figuring out how to translate our strategy to code was a mental exercise we didn't know we needed.

It became a game. How quickly could we code a strategy, or could we turn a complex rule into a simple code? How simple could we make the code without compromising effectiveness?

It's pretty obvious that coding is our favorite part of algorithmic trading.

In this section, we'll give you a simple 8-step method to getting your trading strategy up and running!

For this example, we'll be trading Amazon stock CFD using a simple trading algorithm. The strategy we'll be using involves buying the 'dip in prices.' What this means is that the algorithm will enter long trades when the stocks fall in value in the short term.

Here are the steps:

1. **Choose your product/financial asset.**

   In this example, we've chosen to work with Amazon stock CFD. CFD means contract for difference, and it's essentially a derivative that mimics the price point movements of the actual stock.

2. **Choose your preferred trading software.**

   Depending on how complex the software you've chosen is to install and how much RAM you have, this shouldn't take too much time.

   The software we'll be using for this example is MetaTrader 4 (MT4). We chose this software because it's super beginner-friendly, which makes it easier to use. The learning curve is also pretty flat, so if you decide to go with this software, it shouldn't take you too long to get the hang of it.

The one downside we noticed was that this software isn't great for running complex statistical analysis or machine learning. While we don't think this is something that you should worry about in the early stages of developing your first algorithm, it is something you should keep in mind.

Now, once you've downloaded your preferred software, all you have to do is open the installer and follow the instructions.

3. **Open an account with your preferred broker.**

Once you've successfully installed your software, go to the website of your preferred online or discount broker and set up a demo account.

Now, this may be an issue if your preferred broker doesn't offer demo accounts. If this is the case, we'd recommend you go with the next best broker that does offer demo accounts.

The point here is to get your algorithm up and running to see if it works effectively. Think of this as a test run before the real deal. Therefore, you won't need an actual account for your first run-through.

Depending on the broker you choose, you might need to input certain personal details. This might feel a bit risky. However, if you've done your due diligence and have chosen a reputable and respected broker, you'll have nothing to worry about.

Depending on the types of Demo accounts available, you might get to choose between a standard or premium account. Since we're just doing a test run, we recommend that you go with the standard account.

Now that you've set up your demo account, you should be given your login details.

Next, you'll want to open your trading software and find the tab that says "Login to Trade Account." With MT4, this function is under the "File" tab.

Click on this function and enter your new account details.

4. Understand the strategy.

As mentioned above, in this example, we'll be using a strategy that aims to buy stock once the stock dips. However, the algorithm isn't going to understand what we mean if we just type in "Buy stock when it dips."

So, in this case, we'll have to figure out what a dip means. How much does the stock have to drop to have dipped, and what duration of time should it have 'dipped' for?

It might sound like we're unnecessarily complicating things, but these are aspects you'll need to be clear on before you begin to code.

For this example, let's say that the algorithm will enter a trade when the price of the stock drops lower than its lowest price in the last 15 trading days.

Why 15 days? It really doesn't matter. You'll be able to refine this time frame during backtesting and optimization to get a number that works for you.

Now, with this exercise, we'll be going with the method of spending all the money in the account in order to buy up the max amount of shares possible each time we're able to trade.

Keep in mind that this is a very aggressive approach, and we really don't recommend it for live trading, but since our demo account gives us a bunch of fake money, let's go wild!

At this point, we'll only hold one trade at a time.

When closing the trade, we've programmed the algorithm to exit (sell) once the stock price moves up by 25% (a profit) or if the price moves down by 10% (a loss).

For example, if we enter the trade at a price point of $200, we would close the trade at either $250, making a $50 profit, or $180, thus making a loss of $20.

5. **Understand and set up your trading software.**

   Because this trading strategy is so simple and essentially governed by two fundamental rules, we won't need to use every aspect or feature of MT4.

   Generally, the more complex your strategy is, the more aspects you might need to use. However, the features you'll make use of will depend on the information you need to analyze.

   For this example, we'll be focusing on three features; namely, increasing the chart size, collecting the price data of the stock, and downloading the robot template into the trading software.

   Again, depending on your strategy, these steps will change. In addition, depending on your software, the steps to be able to do this will change.

   Once you've done this, you'll need to understand the parts of your software trading algorithm.

   Aspects that you should understand include what programming language you'll need to code in.

6. **Code your strategy.**

   Unfortunately, it would take way too long to go through an algorithmic trading code line by line, and so,we'll just be going over the basics.

That being said, there are numerous online coding courses that you can take in order to get a more in-depth explanation of coding.

Now, code is read and runs, from top to bottom.

For this trading strategy, the structure of our code would be:

Ask if the price of the stock is lower than the lowest price in the last 15 trading days

Ask price of stock < lowest price in the last 15 trading days (replace lower than with the < symbol)

Ask < lowest price in the last 15 trading days (replace ask price of stock with Ask)

Then we'll have *Ask < iLow(Symbol(), 0, (the data point contains the lowest price in the last 15 trading days))* // iLow() is a function that will give me the low price of a particular data point.

The first input will be the asset that we're working with. The second will be the time frame which is represented by 0. The third is the data point ID that we'll get for the low price.

The code would then be *Ask < iLow(Symbol(), 0, (iLowest(Symbol(), 0, MODE_LOW, 15, 1)))* // iLowest()

Now, the leap from iLow() and iLowest() can seem strange. After all, how are you supposed to know that you should code that?

The simple answer is that you wouldn't know.

When you start learning a new programming language, knowing what code to substitute for certain instructions can be tricky. That's okay. You don't need to know everything at once. If you don't know, Google it! Consult the coding forums.

Now, once your code is complete, all you need to do is compile it. When compiling a code, the program checks the code for any errors and creates a version of the code that your computer is able to understand.

7. Run a historical test with your code.

If your code comes back error-free, it's time to run tests!

The trading software you have installed should have a *Strategy Tester* function.

Side note: when completing these steps, we really advise that you try to find an in-depth, step-by-step video guide and follow along. Make sure that the video is using the safe software as you are. In our experience, we find learning by doing easier than just reading instructions from a page.

Once you have the Strategy Tester up and running, you can set the earliest date as your start date. Remember, you'll be using historical data to run the test!

And, just like that, the first backtest has been completed! Well done! Have a chocolate bar!

At this point, you can check the Report function to see how your algorithm did.

8. **Run it live with fake money.**

Running the algorithm live on the demo account is probably one of our favorite parts of testing code since it'll give you the best idea of whether your algorithm will work or not.

Depending on which broker you've decided to go with, you should have around $100,000 to $200,000 of virtual money to mess around with. Again, this money isn't real, so don't worry about losing it.

The first thing you want to do is open the Terminal Tab and check how much "cash" you have. Once you've done this, run the algorithm by clicking the Enable Automated Trading function.

Then, you'll want to attach the stock price chart to the algorithm (this is key information that your algorithm will need to process in order to execute trades).

And that's it! You're live!

All that's left to do is let it run and see how well you do.

Backtesting and Optimization

Depending on how well your algorithm does during the 'live testing,' you might want to revisit the code and work out any kinks and bugs.

During backtesting and optimization, you need to ensure that your code is operating exactly the way you want it to. During this time, you might also want to rethink your strategy and tweak the code so that it runs more effectively.

This could include changing the time frame, adjusting the input and variables, or fiddling with how you've coded the rules and instructions.

The aim here is to make the algorithm run as efficiently as possible.

However, a word of warning, be careful that you don't end up over-optimizing the algorithm. We've mentioned this before, but if your algorithm is too closely based on historical data, it might cause unnecessary losses since future market trends rarely follow past trends exactly.

Going Live

We know we've spoken about going live before, but that was in reference to a demo or paper trading account.

Once you've thoroughly tested your algorithm and are confident that it will work as intended, it's time to begin using real money. That's right; it's time to remove the kid gloves and start trading.

Now, as with any form of trading, there are risks involved, and this is something you'll need to keep in mind. You might also experience a few emotional ups and downs since your money will be on the line, but this is an exciting time.

Finally, you'll be able to reap the benefits of all your hard work and effort. But, before you get too excited, remember to start small. Don't put all your money into a single stock or asset.

When you're starting with live trade, take it slow and feel things out. During this time, it's also important that you constantly monitor your algorithm and market trends to see how they're performing and to check whether any adjustments are needed.

Maintenance

For as long as your algorithm is running within the statistical parameters you've instructed it to, leave the algorithm alone. While you should monitor the activity in your trading profile to ensure that it's operating correctly, don't mess with the algorithm unnecessarily.

Remember, one of the key benefits of having a trading algorithm is that human emotion doesn't hinder the trading process.

Once the algorithm is up and running, the only thing you need to do is maintain it. Monitor its performance and, if the market shifts, adjust the code accordingly.

The key here is knowing which market conditions your algorithm thrives under and which market conditions might break it down. You'll also need to understand when to leave the algorithm alone and when to intervene.

Finding a balance is tricky, and it'll take some trial and error before you're comfortable doing this. What's important is that you don't give up.

Chapter 4:
Algorithmic Trading Strategies

I've touched on algorithmic trading strategies and the importance of clearly understanding and outlining your strategy before coding in previous chapters. However, the subject of trading strategies is so important that we knew it required a chapter specifically dedicated to it.

There are a vast amount of trading strategies out there, almost as many as there are people, if not more. After all, anyone—and we do mean anyone— can develop a trading strategy completely unique to their characteristics and needs.

That being said, if we were to cover every trading strategy in every form of trade in existence, we'd be here until we were both old and gray.

So, for this chapter, we have narrowed down the field and selected the most prevalent and most popular trading strategies among algorithmic traders.

In this chapter, we'll be covering two main topics: the first is algorithmic trading strategy opportunities, and the second is algorithmic trading strategies.

If you're completely new to trading, we would suggest you pay special attention to this chapter, especially if you haven't quite figured out which strategies you'd like to try. Who knows, you might find your ideal strategy in the next few pages!

Algorithmic Trading Strategy Opportunities

So, what exactly do we mean when we say 'algorithmic trading strategy opportunities'? Well, the idea is quite simple. What we are asking ourselves (and what we think you should be asking yourself) is what opportunities are open to us if we were to begin algorithmic trading? And what opportunities lie in the strategies we could implement?

In essence, how can algorithmic trading broaden your horizons?

Well, in terms of broadening your horizons, learning how to code gives you a fancy skill to add to your resume and opens up a whole new world of possibility (Smigel, 2019). With how tech-focused our society has become, being able to code is an invaluable skill.

In addition to this, being able to write your own algorithms means that you can potentially become a pretty profitable algorithmic trader and begin earning a passive income.

In terms of algorithmic trading strategies, there are two major areas of opportunity, namely, in the strategies used and the markets that you decide to trade in (Smigel, 2019).

The biggest market opportunities that are available for algorithmic traders are to play a role in a space where institutional traders are constrained by capacity and where the data is easy to access and plentiful.

If you'd like to exploit these opportunities, we'd suggest you stay away from competitive markets like high-frequency trading.

The second opportunity is in the strategies you use. Algorithmic trading strategies generally fall into six categories.

- **Quantitative:**

  Quantitative trading strategies, as the name implies, are based on quantitative analysis. Quantitative analyses are basically mathematical computations and equations used to identify trading opportunities.

  These generally involve indicators like volume and price. A quantitative analysis then uses these indicators as inputs for the equations.

- **Mean reversion:**

  Mean reversion strategies run on the belief that the asset price volatility is temporary and will revert back to the historical mean or average price.

  Traders who use this strategy attempt to capitalize on the price of an asset once it returns to its historical average.

- **Trend-following:**

  Trend trading or trend following involves capitalizing on the perceived momentum of an asset. For example, if an asset's price is moving in a certain direction (whether up or down), it is considered a trend.

Traders might then hope to capitalize on this trend by buying as the asset is rising and then selling before the trend inevitably ends.

- **Breakout or Breakdown:**

  Breakout trading involves taking a position on an asset during the early stages of a trend. Generally, this is once an asset's price begins to rise. The aim here is to enter early and close your position once the trend begins to stagnate with the goal of generating as much profit as possible.

- **Arbitrage:**

  Arbitrage trading strategies involve simultaneously buying and selling the same asset across various markets with the aim of making a profit from the minuscule differences in the asset's listed price.

- **Rebalancing exploitation:**

  Traders who use this method aim to generate profits by capitalizing on profile rebalancing.

In addition, there are multiple execution strategies that aim to achieve the best order prices, and these are:

- Tinge-weighted average price (TWAP)
- Volume-weighted average price (VWAP)
- Percentage of volume (POV).

In this chapter, we'll be exploring each of these strategies.

Algorithmic Trading Strategies

The basis of any trading strategy is to identify an opportunity that's still profitable after taking your characteristics and financial profile into consideration. The following are popular algorithmic trading strategies.

Trend-following (Momentum-based) Strategies

Trend-following strategies, also known as momentum-based strategies, are trading strategies that aim to buy financial assets that seem to be on the rise and then selling these assets once their price has peaked (Barone, 2020).

Let's say that there's a particular trend in the market. As a trader or investor, you choose to follow this trend. In this case, traders and investors will analyze the statistical data to determine whether the trend is likely to continue.

Using this information, they'll decide when to sell the asset.

The idea is to take advantage of market volatility by finding buying opportunities that display short-term upward trends and then quickly sell once the asset has lost its momentum.

Commonly used indicators within momentum-based trading are moving averages, price point movements, and channel breakouts.

Trend-based strategies are often the easiest to code and implement via an algorithm because they don't depend on any price forecasts or predictions. The trades you make are based on the emergence of favorable market trends, and these are pretty straightforward to implement via algorithms.

Timing is vital within momentum-based trading because you need to know exactly when to buy and sell in order to avoid a loss and generate profit. This requires that you implement proper risk management techniques.

Therefore, a downside to momentum trading is that it requires proper monitoring, which could take up some of your time. In addition, if you decide to try momentum-based trading, we'd suggest you diversify your trade portfolio to safeguard against potential losses.

Now, there are two main kinds of momentum-based trading strategies. These strategies are either based on past returns or on what's called earnings surprise. Both of these aim to exploit the market reaction to various pieces of information.

- Earnings momentum strategies involve earning a profit from a market under-reaction to information linked to short-term earnings.

- Price momentum strategies involve earning a profit by exploiting the slow market responses to a larger set of information that includes the longer-term profitability of an asset.

Arbitrage Opportunities

Arbitrage opportunities involve foreign exchange and allow traders and investors to earn a profit by simultaneously buying and selling the same security, currency, or commodity across two different markets (Bloomenthal, 2019).

Essentially, the trader buys a dual-listed financial asset at a low price in one market while simultaneously selling that asset at a higher price in a different market. For example, you could buy Amazon stock at $40 in one stock market and then sell that stock in a different market (different region/country) for $100 and make a $60 profit.

It's also common for traders to exploit the arbitrage by buying and selling stock on a foreign exchange where the price hasn't yet been adjusted to the shifting exchange rate.

This method can be used for futures, options, commodities, currency pairs, and stocks.

This trading strategy is great for intermediate traders because it's very simple and should be simple to code. It's also considered low-risk, especially when compared to other trading strategies.

That being said, there are various sub-strategies within arbitrage that can be more complex. One such method focuses on keeping an eye on corporate events such as acquisition, company mergers, or the launch of a new company venture as triggers for investment and trade (Bhagat & Singh, 2018).

Traders and investors will then make moves depending on the perceived outcome of these corporate events.

Another popular method is statistical arbitrage.

Statistical Arbitrage:

Statistical Arbitrage occurs when an arbitrage opportunity emerges due to a misquote of the price point of the asset. This method can be very profitable when used in conjunction with algorithmic trading.

The aim here is to profit from the mispricing of the financial instrument based on the expected value of the financial instrument (Bhagat & Singh, 2018).

This method also works well with algorithmic trading because of how quickly you'll need to enter and exit positions due to market fluctuations. While it might be quite difficult for a human to keep up the pace and track these price point changes, an algorithm will have no such problems.

Statistical Arbitrage Algorithms are heavily based on mean revisions and work best when using the pair trading strategy. **Pair trading** is a statistical arbitrage strategy that focuses on stocks that have shown historical co-movement in prices. These stocks are pairs based on fundamental and market-based similarities.

Pair trading works with the idea that the relative prices in market exchanges exist in equilibrium and that any deviations to this rule would eventually correct themselves.

Therefore, when one stock outperforms another, it's believed that the outperformer was sold short, and the underperformer was bought long. This short-term divergence will eventually end with the prices matching up.

Let's use Pepsi and Coke as an example. Both are huge soda companies that sell pretty similar products. Historically, these companies have shared price dips and increases. Therefore, if the price of Pepsi increased significantly, while Coke stayed the same, pair traders would buy up Coke stock and sell their Pepsi stock with the assumption that the stock prices will return to their historic balance point.

If they're right, they'll earn a profit from the difference in price points from both the Pepsi and Coke stock.

While this is a pretty straightforward method, and with the right coding could lead to profit, you'll need a lot of starting capital to do arbitrage. You'll also need access to the latest technology and have the necessary expertise to make arbitrage profitable.

Index Fund Rebalancing

Before we get into index fund rebalancing, let's define what rebalancing is and how it works.

Rebalancing involves realigning a trade or investment portfolio in terms of how the assets are weighted. The purpose is to buy and sell assets in order to bring the portfolio back to the desired asset distribution.

For example, let's say your goal was to trade 20% stocks, 50% commodities, and 30% futures contracts.

However, over time, you've ended up trading 50% stocks and 50% futures contracts, and your trading portfolio no longer looks the way you want it to look.

Depending on whether your trading strategy and financial aims have changed, you may decide to rebalance your portfolio so that you can reach your target allocation of 20%, 50%, 30%.

Rebalancing your portfolio also safeguards you from being exposed to unnecessary risks by ensuring that your portfolio remains sufficiently diversified and that you continue to operate within your area of expertise (Chen, 2019b).

Now, this is all good and well, but how are you supposed to make a profit from rebalancing?

Well, with index fund rebalancing, traders aim to rebalance their portfolios so that it's in line with their benchmark indices. Algorithmic traders can take advantage of this by capitalizing on the trades.

These trades could possibly offer 20 to 80 basis point profits depending on how many stocks are in the fund before it's rebalanced. Algorithmic trading works well here because the program is able to execute these trades at the correct time to ensure the best possible prices (Planning and Executing Index Rebalance Trades | Ryedale, 2021).

Quantitative-based Strategies

Quantitative trading involves trading strategies that are rooted in quantitative analysis. These kinds of trading strategies are also known as **mathematical**

model-based strategies and are dependent on mathematical functions and equations to pick out trading opportunities (Sharma, 2021). When using mathematical model-based strategies, backtesting becomes vital when trying to pick out these trade opportunities.

Quantitative trading is quite innovative and exploits modern technology, the availability of data and information, and mathematics in order to trade profitably.

Generally, traders will take a trading strategy that they've resonated with and use it as the basis to create a mathematical model. Then, they'll develop an algorithm that tests this model on historical market data (Sharma, 2021).

The model will be backtested numerous times until it's been optimized to function the way the trader intends it to.

Think of it this way: let's say the weatherman processes a report and predicts an 80% chance of rain while the sun is still out. The weatherman could've come to this conclusion by collecting and analyzing climate data from the surrounding area and found that historically, this area receives rain 80 out of 100 times.

Therefore, he can state with confidence that there is an 80% chance of rain due to the results of his data analysis.

Quantitative trade strategies operate on a similar concept by using mathematical equations to analyze market data like volume, correlation to other assets, and historical price point movements in order to develop or verify a trading strategy.

A downside to quantitative trade is that your trading model has to align with financial market conditions. Therefore, there is a risk that, if the market shifts, your model might be rendered useless, and you'll have to start all over again.

Trading Range (Mean Reversion) Trading Strategies

Trading range strategies are based on the idea that price fluctuations of a financial instrument are inherently temporary and will eventually return to their average value in time (Chen, 2021).

By spotting and outlining a price range and developing an algorithm based on that price range allows trades to be executed once the price of the asset leaves this range.

The trading range strategy is often used in the statistical analysis of market conditions. This concept can also be applied to options price when describing the price volatility of an asset and how it fluctuates around a long-term average (Chen, 2021).

The best way to implement this strategy is to use it in conjunction with various forecasting techniques. The idea is that, by using these strategies and techniques simultaneously, traders will be able to spot the best possible trade opportunities.

Think of it this way: let's say when analyzing historical data, you find that the average price of a stock is $50 and that it fluctuates pretty regularly from $55 to $44. When coding this, you'll want your algorithm to have access to historical data as well as price point charts and mean average charts.

Using these inputs, you'd want your algorithm to buy stock when the price drops below $50 and sell stock once the price goes above $50, thus profiting from the price difference.

If you're well versed in reading market trends and have an effective trading algorithm in place, the mean reversion strategy could be pretty profitable. That being said, as with every strategy in trade, the mean reversion strategy is not without risk.

A major risk with this method is that you can't be 100% sure that the normal price fluctuation pattern will occur as you've predicted. Sometimes market exchanges can fluctuate unexpectedly, which could cause unforeseen highs and lows.

These events could be triggered by the release of a new product, a company merger, or the emergence of another prominent competitor.

Volume-weighted Average Price (VWAP)

Volume-weighted average price (VWAP) is a trading benchmark used by traders when trying to determine the average price of a financial asset that has been traded throughout the day. As the name suggests, the

VWAP is based on the volume and price of the asset (Fernando, 2021).

Traders generally use this information to gain insight into market trends and the value of the asset.

VWAP breaks up a large order and releases the smaller chunks of the order to the market by using stock-specific historical volume profiles (Fernando, 2021). This is done with the aim to execute a trade that's as close to the VWAP as possible.

This strategy is often implemented when traders want a smoothed out indication of an asset's price over a specific period of time. It can also be used by more prominent traders when they want to ensure that their trades don't go above the price that they want to buy or sell at.

Calculating the VWAP of an asset is pretty simple. Using the VWAP, one can calculate the amount traded for every transaction and then dividing this amount by the total shares traded.

A major limitation of VWAP-based trading strategies is that VWAP is a single-day indicator. What this means is that the VWAP benchmark is restarted at the beginning of each trading day. This limits its uses, especially for algorithmic trading, because the average VWAP over a period of time is likely not accurate to the true VWAP reading (Fernando, 2021).

The VWAP is also based on historical data and, thus, is not inherently predictive.

That being said, we wouldn't recommend VWAP-based trading strategies to beginners since it can be pretty complicated to code and requires a working knowledge of market trends and financial markets.

Time-weighted Average Price (TWAP)

Time-weighted average price (TWAP) is based on the weighted average price within a particular period of time. Much like the VWAP, the TWAP is a trading algorithm that's used when traders want to execute a large number of trades.

When using the TWAP, traders are able to split a large order into numerous small orders that are valued at the TWAP price. This is done with the aim to prevent large orders from suddenly increasing the value of a financial asset in market exchanges.

Let us put it this way: executing an order for 10,000 shares will have a much larger impact on the price of those shares than, say, 100 small orders of 1,000 shares will. Larger orders, when executed, temporarily push up the value of an asset, which won't work in the trader's favor if he aims to buy.

In essence, TWAP is used to divide large orders into smaller orders in order to make trading easier for traders and investors.

TWAP can also be used by traders when they're trying to find the value of the market price of an asset. It's most commonly used by high-volume or high-frequency traders.

Calculating TWAP is pretty simple. All you need to do is average the entire day's price bar (open, high, low, and the closing prices for that day). And then, based on the time that you decided to execute the order, every day's average price is taken in order to calculate the average of the entire duration's prices.

The equation looks like this:

Average of each day's price = (Open + Close + High + Low prices) / 4

TWAP differs from the above-mentioned VWAP in that VWAP cannot be calculated as easily as TWAP. TWAP is also defined by time, whereas VWAP is defined by volume.

As simple as TWAP is to calculate, it's not without its flaws. A few downsides to this trading strategy is that it can often be too predictable, and this can leave your strategy vulnerable to other traders. This method of trade isn't sophisticated and lacks a lot of the nuances of other trading strategies mentioned in this chapter.

Percentage of Volume (POV)

The percentage of volume (POV) trading strategy, also known as the participant strategy, focuses on controlling the pace of trade execution by targeting the percentage of the market volume (*Percent of Volume (POV)*, n.d.). This is done to ensure that trade stays as close to the POV as possible.

The POV trading strategy thus aims to trade at a clearly defined percentage of the current market volume until the order set out by the trader has been completed or until the financial market closes.

When used in conjunction with algorithmic trading, your algorithm will continuously send out partial orders based on the participation/percentage ratio that you've set until the order has been completed.

So, this method of trade is most beneficial if you plan to execute high-volume trades or large orders within a specific window of time. It's also commonly used when traders are satisfied with the expected market price since POV executes trades close to market price.

Much like with TWAP, POV can also be used if traders want to limit the impact larger orders might have on the price of the asset.

Now, when implementing POV, there are a few strategy parameters you should consider. The parameters you actually end up using will depend on your trading strategy and the broker you've chosen to go with.

The first parameter you should be aware of is the start time. The **start time** determines whether or not an order will be sent to the market exchange. Therefore, you should be aware of what the start time of your market is to prevent incurring unnecessary losses. The start time will vary from financial market to financial market and from broker to broker.

The second parameter is the end time. Much like the start time, the **end time** determines whether or not an order will be executed.

The third parameter is **percentage volume**. POV, when coded into an algorithm, will automatically adjust the participation rate of your trades in order to limit the percentage of the asset's total traded volume. For example, if an asset is being traded at 100,000 shares per minute and the percentage volume is 20%, the algorithm will trade 20,000 shares a minute.

Basically, the percentage volume dictates how many shares are traded within a specific period of time.

The fourth parameter is the **price brand**. You can think of the price brand as the price limit that you can set on an asset. If the market price moves beyond the price brand limit, the algorithm won't execute the order.

The last parameter is the **reference price**. Much like the price brand, the reference price influences the price that the algorithm will execute trades at. Depending on how you've coded your algorithm, it should automatically try to beat the reference price when executing trades in order to earn larger profits.

Implementation Shortfall

Implementation shortfall is a trading strategy that focuses on the differences between the current price of an asset when a buy or sell decision is made and the final execution price after taking into consideration additional trade fees such as taxes and commissions (Hayes, 2020).

This is usually caused by a time lag between making the trade and completing it and could be due to the poor network or internet connection.

Therefore, the implementation shortfall is the sum of the execution costs and the initial (opportunity) costs should the market fluctuate between the time the order was opened and when it was closed. This is also known as a slippage.

An implementation shortfall trading strategy aims to maximize the profits earned by the trader by reducing the cost of execution. This is done by trading on real-time market exchanges. Doing this saves on not only the cost of the order but also the opportunity cost that could be incurred on a delayed execution.

Recent technological developments that have helped to minimize costs include the introduction of real-time quotes and the general move of brokers toward commission-free trading.

Additional methods you can use to minimize implementation shortfalls are using limit orders or stop-limit orders instead of market orders. Unlike market orders, a limit order will only fill at the price you want it to or a better price than the one you've set. Therefore, the order won't fill at a lower price than what you were expecting (Hayes, 2020).

A possible downside of using limit and stop-limit orders is that you might miss out on pretty lucrative opportunities. We would also advise that you only use limit and stop-limit orders when the market is favorable since they can prevent you from quickly exiting positions if the market becomes volatile.

That being said, as much as we'd like to completely eliminate this aspect of trading, implementation shortfalls are inevitable.

Sentiment-based Trading Strategies

Now, we've briefly touched on sentiment-based trading in previous chapters. In this section, we'll be doing an in-depth dive into this trading strategy and how it works.

As discussed, market sentiment is when investors or traders in general move toward or away from a particular financial instrument or market (Smith, 2019). It's a general consensus about a particular financial instrument, either a negative consensus or a positive consensus. Generally, market sentiments are positive.

Market sentiments can be seen when looking at price movements of assets. Rapidly rising prices indicate a positive market sentiment (bullish) and rapidly falling prices indicate a negative market sentiment (bearish).

Unlike the other trading strategies mentioned in this chapter, market sentiment isn't always based on fundamentals, market trends, or data and news feeds (Smith, 2019). Oftentimes, market sentiment is driven by human emotion. It's driven by the fear of missing out on lucrative opportunities.

Technical indicators that can be used to measure market sentiment are the High-Low Index, the Bullish Percent Index (BPI), the CBOE Volatility Index (VIX), and moving averages.

Market sentiment is often used by day traders because it directly influences the technical indicators that day traders use when measuring and deciding on what to trade in order to profit from short-term price point movements.

Market sentiment can also be used by contrarian investors who aim to go against the crowd in the belief that the market will naturally correct itself once the sentiment disappears.

If they're experienced, traders and investors are also able to profit from market sentiment if they happen upon an under-or overvalued financial asset and are able to act quickly.

A major advantage of market sentiment is that you'll have to get a pretty good idea of how customers are feeling about a particular company and product. If the market has shifted toward a company, chances are they favor that company and expect it to do well. If the market has shifted away from a particular company, it's likely that they don't have much faith that the company will do well.

Market Making

A market maker (whether a firm or an individual trader) acts on both sides of the market when trading. What this means is that they provide bids and offers (asks) as well as sell financial instruments to the best offer. In this way, they're able to act on both sides of the market.

For example, let's say that a market maker is trading in Apple stocks, and they offer a quote of $20.00 -

$20.05, 100x500. This means that they'll bid (buy) 100 shares for $20, and they'll offer (sell) 500 shares for $20.05, thus earning a profit from the difference between the bid price and the offer price.

Other traders and investors are then able to buy (lift the offer) the stock from the market marker at $20.05 or sell shares to them (hit the bid) for $20.

Once a market maker receives an order from another trader, they'll immediately sell shares from their holdings.

An interesting aspect about market makers is that they're somewhat shielded from the usual risks that come along with trading because they're able to offer two-way quotes in the market.

That being said, market makers still face the risk of having their securities and assets decline in value after they have been bought and before they've had a chance to sell it. After all, if the selling price is lower than the buying price, they'll make a loss.

One of the main purposes of market makers, as the name suggests, is to help make the market operate more efficiently by increasing market liquidity. They also earn a profit from the difference between the bid-ask spread.

Market makers are able to increase market liquidity by buying and selling quotations for a specific amount of assets. This can be stock, commodities, futures, or options, any financial instrument really.

In most cases, market makers are employed by larger financial firms or by the market exchange for the sole purpose of increasing the liquidity of financial markets and trade volume into financial assets.

Chapter 5:
Evaluating and Monitoring Your Algorithms

We know we've touched on the importance of monitoring and evaluating your algorithms once they're up and running. However, we have yet to give you tips on how to do so.

As we mentioned before, properly monitoring and evaluating your algorithms is an essential step for any algorithmic trader, no matter their skill and experience level.

For algorithmic traders, their success in trading is completely dependent on whether or not their algorithms are able to operate efficiently. In addition, their strategies and systems also need to be adaptable to variance since market conditions are often in flux and dependent on the underlying economic environment.

Market conditions, exchanges, and trends are also always changing and can behave in unpredictable ways. Therefore, it's important to ensure that the algorithm that you've programmed is updated to remain compatible with current market conditions and trends.

One of the key reasons to evaluate and monitor the

performance of your algorithm is to ensure that it remains up to date and doesn't become irrelevant and incompatible with the financial market that you're working in.

In this chapter, we'll be giving you a few pointers on how to check if your algorithm is still able to keep up with market trends and perform well, as well as how to know when it needs to be updated.

Evaluating Trading Strategies

Technological development and innovation have progressed in leaps and bounds in recent years, and this has been golden for algorithmic and systematic traders. Not only have these technological developments drastically changed the landscape of finance, trade, and investment, they have also made the process incredibly easy and user-friendly.

One area that has been improved is evaluating and monitoring algorithms. Current market analysis platforms have made it incredibly simple for algorithmic traders to review their trading systems.

Evaluating and monitoring your algorithm has become as simple as compiling a strategy performance report and judging whether or not the algorithm still meets your trading and financial needs.

Strategy performance reports are compiled by applying performance metrics to your algorithm and are essentially a compilation of different datasets based on various mathematical aspects of your algorithm's performance (Folger, 2019). This report is essentially an objective overview of how your algorithm has performed within the financial market exchange. Analyzing the strategy performance report of your algorithm is a great way of finding the strengths and weaknesses in your algorithm.

Think of it as a tool to help you find what's working in your algorithm and what isn't. This tool can be used when backtesting and using historical data, as well as when your algorithm goes live.

For algorithmic traders, strategy performance reports are invaluable. Most market analysis platforms offer this feature to traders, particularly during backtesting. Most online brokers should offer this feature as well, although it might be hidden behind a paywall.

Key Components of a Strategy Performance Report

When analyzing a strategy performance report, you should be familiar with the general format the report will take and how you should read it. Now, in our experience, strategy performance reports have a pretty standard format all around. However, there might be slight differences depending on which online broker or market analyst platforms you've chosen.

Some brokers and market analyst platforms might have different methods of displaying data, and it might take a few tries to get the hang of them.

That being said, there are a few basic components of a strategy performance report that you should familiarize yourself with.

Front Page (Summary)

The front page of the strategy performance report is essentially a summary of the performance metrics and the rest of the data in the report. It's a snapshot of how your algorithm has performed in the financial market over a specific period of time.

This information is commonly displayed in a table format with the performance metrics listed on the left of the table and the corresponding calculations listed to the right of the table.

Key Performance Metrics

Key performance metrics that should be listed in both the summary and within the report are the *total net profits*, the *percentage profitable*, *average trade net profit, profit factor,* and *the maximum drawdown*. As you can probably tell, these metrics are good indicators of how well your algorithm is performing.

It's very likely that your strategy performance report will contain a plethora of data, statistics, and information. However, these metrics are the most relevant when evaluating performance.

Performance metrics are usually illustrated using graphs that display the trade data of each metric over a specific period of time.

These metrics are a great starting point for beginners who are still getting the hang of analyzing data and implementing trade strategies. They're also great if you want an initial scope of the performance of your algorithm before diving into the rest of the data.

But what do these key metrics mean? Here is a quick breakdown:

1. Total Net Profits

The total net profit is essentially the bottom line or the ultimate goal of a trading system over a specific period of time. After all, the goal of trade is to generate profit, and this performance metric tells you how much net profit you've earned.

The total net profits are calculated by subtracting the gross loss of all trades (this includes any trade fees such as commissions or holding fees) from the gross profits of all successful trades. The equation should look something like this:

> Gross Profits - (Gross Loss + Trade Fees) = Total Net Profits

The total net profits metric is a great indicator of performance and the viability of both your trading strategy and your algorithm; however, it cannot be viewed in isolation. Trusting this metric alone can be quite deceptive since it isn't an accurate indicator of whether your algorithm is actually performing effectively.

This indicator is also unable to normalize the results of the algorithm when taking into consideration the amount of risk involved.

Therefore, while an invaluable metric, we would strongly advise against reading it in isolation.

2. Percentage Profitable

The percentage profitable indicates the probability of your algorithm to execute successful trades. Unlike with the previous performance metric, there isn't one ideal value that every trader should aspire to. Instead, the 'ideal value' varies from trader to trader, depending on your trade style and strategy.

When trend trading, traders will often have a lower percentage profitable value because they typically execute larger trades that involve potentially large profits. This is because successful trades generate huge profits.

When using this method of trade, the percentage profitable value can be as low as 40%, and yet, the trader might still be wildly successful due to the large gains. Trades that are unsuccessful are also usually closed at a small loss when compared to the gains.

The percentage profitable is calculated with the following equation:

> (Successful Trades ÷ Total Number of Trades) x 100 = Percentage Profitable

3. Average Trade Net Profit

The average trade net profit refers to the average amount of money that you gained or lost per trade. This performance metric considers both successful and unsuccessful trades and is based on the total net profit metric discussed earlier.

A downside of this metric is that it can easily be skewed by an outlier. For example, a single trade that generated a much larger profit when compared to the others can throw off the average trade net profit. This can result in an overinflated average trade net profit value that can make you seem much more profitable than you really are.

To avoid this, you could remove the outlier from the equation for a more accurate value.

The average trade net profit is calculated as follows:

Total Net Profits ÷ Total Number of Trades = Average Trade Net Profit

4. Profit Factor

The profit factor is the gross profit divided by the gross losses (+trade fees). This metric considers all trades conducted during an entire trading period. This is done in order to find out the amount of profit you generate per unit of risk.

The profit factor is calculated as follows:

Total Gross Profits ÷ (Total Gross Losses + Trade Fees) = Profit Factor

However, unlike with the percentage profitable, there is an ideal value that you should aim for.

For example, let's say your total gross profits are $149,020, and your gross losses combined with your trading fees are around $75,215. When using the calculation, you should have a profit factor of 1.98.

Now, 1.98 is a very reasonable profit factor and is an indicator that your trading algorithm generates a profit. While risks and losses are inherent in trade, your goal should be to offset those losses and the potential risk by consistently generating a profit.

By using the profit factor, you'll know just how much your profits outweigh your losses.

If your profit factor is below 1, for example, a 0.94, this means that your gross losses exceed your gross profits, and therefore your algorithm isn't successfully generating profits. In this case, we would strongly advise that you reevaluate your algorithm and trading strategy.

5. **Maximum Drawdown**

The maximum drawdown is essentially the 'worst-case scenario' for a trading period (Folger, 2019). This performance metric helps traders measure the amount of risk they might sustain because of the algorithm. It also helps you figure out whether your algorithm is viable, based on how large the account is.

The basic premise here is that if the amount of cash you're willing to risk is less than the maximum drawdown, it's likely that the trading system you've come up with is not suited for you. In that case, we would advise you to go back to the drawing board and rethink your trading strategy and algorithm.

What makes the maximum drawdown such an essential metric is that it acts as something of a wake-up call, especially to idealistic and newbie traders. This metric needs to align with your risk tolerance and the size of your trading account.

There's nothing wrong with dreaming big and shooting for the stars; however, if you want to achieve your financial goals, they need to be realistic. The same goes for your trading strategy.

Additional Aspects That You Should Evaluate

While the strategy performance report is the main, and possibly the easiest method you could use when evaluating your trading strategy, it shouldn't be the only method you use.

Your strategy performance report is a great way to get a general overview of how your algorithm has been performing. However, if you want to get the full picture, you should consider the following aspects:

1. Methodology

As the name implies, the methodology refers to how, why, where, and when you're implementing your strategy. This aspect focuses on the parameters of your strategy, the market conditions, broker, trading strategy, code, and so forth.

The methodology essentially involves everything you've done up until this point.

When evaluating your methodology, you're basically retracing your steps with the aim of finding out where you might've made mistakes. This means thinking through every step and choice you've made and deciding if they were sound or not.

Now, this might sound like a lot, but it's very simple. When evaluating your methodology, we suggest you use your strategy performance report as a guide.

For example, if your profit factor is low, you can focus on evaluating your trading strategy, as well as your trading fees and expenses. Oftentimes, a low-profit factor could be because you're being charged for hidden fees by your broker.

In this case, your profit factor would be directing you to specific areas of your algorithm and trade that need your attention. All you have to do is rethink your methodology in these areas and pick out the weak points.

2. Frequency

The frequency of your trading strategy refers to how often your algorithm executes trades. Therefore, high-frequency trading means that you'll be executing a lot of trades throughout a trading period, while low-frequency trading means that you're executing a small number of trades throughout a trading period.

High-frequency trading strategies are commonly used by day traders.

Now, high-frequency trading has the potential to generate large profits; however, it also carries the risk of incurring large losses. That being said, one of the things you should consider is whether you're willing to risk enough capital for the number of trades you'd like to execute.

For example, you'll need a lot of capital for high-frequency trading and less capital for low-frequency trading.

A good indicator of this is the maximum drawdown performance parameter mentioned above.

3. Parameters

The parameters of your algorithm and trading strategy are essentially the limitations of your algorithm. Therefore, your algorithm cannot perform beyond the parameters that you've set during coding.

If you refer back to Chapter 3 we discussed knowing the rules of your trading strategy and being able to code those rules. Well, the parameters are those rules. They tell your algorithm how and when to operate. They also limit how much and how often your algorithm executes trades.

If you're having trouble with your algorithm's performance, the first aspect we recommend you check is your rules.

Oftentimes your algorithm might be struggling because of the rules you've set. Perhaps you haven't thought them through properly or coded them correctly. Sometimes, the entire trading strategy is wrong, and you have to go back to the drawing board.

4. Volatility

Volatility refers to the amount of risk associated with a trading strategy. This aspect of your trading strategy and algorithm should be present in the strategy performance report.

This aspect focuses on not only your trading strategy but also the financial asset you'll be trading.

Therefore, the higher the volatility of an underlying asset, the higher the risk of a loss.

The lower the volatility, the lower the risk.

The volatility rate is often illustrated using the Sharpe ratio. The Sharpe ratio was developed by William Sharpe, hence the name, and is used to analyze and understand the return of an investment when compared to the risk (Fernando, 2019).

Generally, the larger the Sharpe ratio, the better the risk-adjustment return. Therefore, when using this calculation, it's best to aim for a higher Sharpe ratio because that would mean that the reward far outweighs the risk.

So, what happens after you've analyzed your strategy performance report? Well, we suppose that answer depends on the results of your report. If the report is favorable and your algorithm and trading strategies are working as intended, there isn't much you need to do.

At this point, you might have decided to tweak your trading strategy a bit in order to make it more effective, but other than minor changes, you should be feeling pretty confident. We know we would be.

On the other hand, if your report has worrying results, your next step is to take an in-depth look at your algorithm and strategy and try to figure out where you might've gone wrong. This could entail doing more backtesting and stress testing, going back and checking the code, or reevaluating current market conditions.

Here are a few steps you can take after evaluating your algorithm:

Determine Whether There's a Need For Change

After you've analyzed your strategy performance report and have gone over all the performance metrics and performance values, you need to determine whether there's a need for a change.

Ask yourself whether it's time to adjust your trading strategy. Is there a genuine need for change? Now, finding the answers to this question isn't that difficult.

Check your strategy performance report. The answers lie within the values you'll find there. Therefore, if the statistics and values are poor, you should probably rethink your strategy. However, if your results are great, then you could think about making a few tweaks, but there isn't much to worry about.

That being said, in our experience, having a new algorithm go live can be quite thrilling. The first time we ran an algorithm live, using real money, our stomachs were twisted for days. We were glued to our PCs, constantly checking and rechecking our algorithm.

You might experience a similar state of anxiety, and this could cause you to evaluate your strategy before your algorithm has had a chance to prove itself.

Our point here is that you have to give it time. Don't rush in with an evaluation until you've given your algorithm a chance to thrive.

As mentioned previously, your trading strategies need to be versatile and be able to operate effectively within the constantly fluctuating market conditions. However, in order to test your algorithm's viability across fluctuating market conditions, you need to give it time.

Figure Out How Much You Need to Adjust

After you've decided whether or not you actually need to adjust your algorithm, you need to figure out how extensive those adjustments need to be. Do you need slight tweaks here and there, maybe shifting a few calculations and a bit of code around, or do you need to overhaul the entire system and start from scratch?

The extent of the adjustments often depends on the performance of your algorithm. A good way to figure out which aspects of your algorithm need adjusting is by looking at your strategy performance report.

In our experience, we've found that checking out the performance metrics is a great way of figuring out where the weaknesses and errors are. In that case, you can pick apart those aspects which might be giving you trouble and make adjustments to them instead of having to overhaul the entire system.

It could also be that there's nothing inherently wrong with your algorithm, and it could just be experiencing system death. System death is when your algorithm is no longer viable or effective within current market exchange conditions.

In this case, you'll have to carefully break apart your

system and find the aspect of your algorithm that no longer serves its purpose. It could be an indicator that has changed or that certain aspects of your algorithm have become ineffective. It could also be that your algorithm lacked true versatility.

Either way, breaking apart your system and analyzing each aspect can be ridiculously time-consuming and frustrating. It's also a difficult method of going about adjusting your algorithm and requires extensive experience and knowledge regarding trade, technical indicators, and coding.

If you're forced to overhaul your algorithm and design and build a new trading system, you'll have to dedicate quite a bit of time to it as well. Overhauling a system takes much more thought, effort, and consideration than just finding and making minor adjustments.

The key point in this section is that you need to be able to pinpoint the weaknesses and strengths of your algorithm by observing your algorithm's performance and the performance metrics. Basically, you need to be able to identify what is working and why, as well as what isn't working and why.

Once you have that figured out, you need to know how extensive your adjustments need to be.

That being said, it's also important to note that fiddling with one aspect of your algorithm has a ripple effect on every other aspect of your algorithm. Therefore, when making minor adjustments, be aware of the effects it's having on the entire system. The worst-case scenario is when you adjust one aspect, and it ends up making your whole algorithm unstable.

Making The Necessary Adjustments and Live Testing

Once you've figured out the issues in your algorithm and you've made the necessary adjustments, it's time to test the system via backtesting and stress testing. Now, we've been over this before, and, once again, the best-simulated tests you can run are on demo accounts or paper trading accounts (*6 Steps to Evaluate Your Trading Strategy for Optimal Performance*, 2019).

However, you should be careful not to get caught in the paper trading phase or try to make your algorithm perfect since this could lead to over-optimization. Getting stuck in paper trading also won't benefit you much if you're trying to learn more about live market operations.

Again, don't be afraid to take your time. With trading, there really is no rush. Trading opportunities will always be available.

What's important in this step is to carefully observe your algorithm's performance metrics while testing and running simulations. It's also wise to run your algorithm through various iterations of the simulation, allowing you to objectively and comprehensively evaluate the viability and effectiveness of the adjustments you've made.

Regular Evaluations

Now, we've mentioned this before, but certain lessons bear repeating. If we lived in an ideal world, all your algorithms would run perfectly without needing intervention, and you would generate enough profit that you'd be able to live off the interest.

Unfortunately, the world is as flawed as we are, and your algorithm might be good, but it won't be perfect (*6 Steps to Evaluate Your Trading Strategy for Optimal Performance*, 2019). Therefore, it's essential that you conduct regular evaluations in order to maintain its efficiency.

If you're able to do this successfully, you should notice considerable improvements when comparing your past strategy performance reports with current and future performance reports.

That being said, it's important to ensure that when evaluating your strategy, you give your algorithm the space and time to settle within the market exchange and prove itself. Then, when evaluating your algorithm, you'll have enough data to work with.

Oftentimes, if you're too early with your evaluation, you'll have a relatively small data sample to work with, and this can cause misleading results.

Iterate

Iteration is key when monitoring and evaluating your algorithm. In fact, we'd go as far as to argue that iteration forms part of every step of developing and running an algorithm.

In short, no matter which part of the process you're in, you'll need to run your algorithm through numerous iterations until you're able to get the desired result. For example, when developing a trading strategy, you might have to test out various iterations of a trading strategy before you settle on one that suits you. When converting that strategy into code, you might also need to test out various iterations of the code before you're able to land on one that works as intended.

The point here is to test and retest and refine your strategy and algorithm until it serves your purpose.

If you're finding trouble with any of these steps, don't be afraid to ask for help. Often, our eyes miss what is very clear to others, so don't be afraid to scroll the forums. Who knows, you might even make a friend!

Monitoring Your Algorithm

When evaluating your algorithm, it's likely that you'll only conduct evaluations after a trading period, or bi-annually. In our experience, evaluations aren't that effective when conducted too frequently.

On the other hand, monitoring your algorithm should be a more frequent activity. Unlike evaluation, monitoring your algorithm doesn't have to be as time-consuming. In most cases, it could entail checking in on your trading account, your trading profile, and your algorithm just to see if it's operating the way it should.

Monitoring your algorithm is vital, especially if you're a beginner or if you're running a new algorithm. The main aim is to ensure that your algorithm is operating as intended, as well as picking up on any possible bugs, weaknesses, or errors in your algorithm.

Having easy access to your trading portfolio and trading account is a great way to monitor the progress and performance of your algorithm. This is also a great way to keep track of all the trades your algorithm is making.

These days, most online and discount brokers offer a mobile app platform that automatically syncs your trading profile and account to your cellphone. You're also able to make trades and manage your account from these apps.

Having a mobile trading app on your cell phone allows you to quickly and easily monitor the performance of your algorithm from wherever you are in the world. All you need is an internet connection.

Mobile trading apps are essential for any trader, whether you have a busy lifestyle or not. They give you the freedom to spend your time as you wish without having to be chained to your PC, executing trades, or monitoring your algorithm.

In our experience, having access to a mobile trading app also took a lot of pressure off our shoulders when we first started with algorithmic trading. It allowed us to peel ourselves from our computer and gave us the comfort of knowing that we could check on our trading profile and account whenever and wherever we wanted.

Therefore, we would advise that, when looking for an online broker, you choose one that offers a great mobile platform. It's also important to ensure that the mobile app is supported by your mobile device.

Chapter 6:
Risk Management

Up until this point, we've mentioned the risks associated with trading and the inherent risks that come along with each trade executed. In the previous chapter, we also went over a few performance metrics, a few of which covered risks when calculating the viability or profitability of trades.

However, thus far, we haven't told you how to manage risks. Notice how we didn't use the word 'avoid' because, while risks can be mitigated and managed, it's impossible to avoid them completely.

Every trade, no matter the method, asset, or strategy, comes with some measure of risk. Unfortunately, in the world of trade and finance, risks are unavoidable. Therefore, it's vital that every trader and investor implement some form of risk management strategy before proceeding.

Now, oftentimes the risk strategies one can employ when trading is inherent in the trade strategies. Think about it. In previous chapters, we've spoken extensively about evaluation, backtesting, and making use of paper trading accounts when testing out new strategies and algorithms.

These steps are essentially a form of risk management. For example, when backtesting, you're ensuring that your trading strategy and algorithm work the way you intend it to. This lessens the risk of incurring unnecessary losses because your algorithm is ineffective.

The same goes for regular monitoring and evaluations.

In this chapter, we'll discuss the risks unique to algorithmic trading, as well as trading in general, and how to manage these risks. We'll also be covering the common mistakes made by newbie traders and how to avoid them.

Risks

There are a plethora of risks associated with trade and investment. There are also different risks associated with different trading strategies and methods. Therefore, one of the first things you'll need to do when deciding on a trading strategy and method is to consider the risks involved.

For example, the risks associated with day trading might be different from the risks associated with swing trading, and high volume trading carries different risks than high-frequency trading.

That being said, there are specific risks associated with algorithmic trading that you should be aware of before you jump in.

High Volatility

As we've discussed before, in order for your algorithm to be effective, it needs to be able to handle changes in market conditions. Not only will you need to be able to anticipate certain market changes, but you'll also need to ensure that your algorithm is flexible enough to handle these changes. Now, coding your algorithm to be able to handle market-related changes is no walk in the park. It requires a good working knowledge of trading and financial market exchanges, as well as great coding skills.

Even if you're able to code a flexible algorithm that's able to handle market changes, there's always the risk that your algorithm might react adversely to market changes by excessively widening the bid-ask spread, or it may stop functioning altogether.

This could lead to increased volatility and a decrease in liquidity. In the worst-case scenario, your algorithm could continue functioning but be executing risky trades due to changing market conditions, thus increasing your losses.

Incorrect Algorithms

Another major risk that algorithmic traders face is implementing a faulty algorithm. This could be because you didn't code a specific instruction correctly, or you haven't thought through your strategy enough. It could also occur if you haven't set clearly defined rules and instructions or if you've misunderstood how a trading strategy operates.

Whatever the reason, an error or weakness in your algorithm could cause an increase in losses over a very short period of time.

While the risk exists, it can be managed by backtesting your algorithm and testing it out on paper trading accounts. However, too much backtesting can lead to over-optimization.

As discussed, over-optimization occurs when your algorithm works amazingly when backtesting yet isn't compatible with current, live market fluctuations and changes. In this case, your algorithm might seem like it works perfectly when conducting backtesting because you've unintentionally fit your algorithm to historical data and market trends instead of live market conditions.

In this case, the performance of your algorithm when backtesting is misleading and won't correlate with its performance in live market exchanges.

Chain Reactions

Global markets have become increasingly integrated due to rapid technological developments in the world of finance. Therefore, when a change occurs in one financial market, the change often ripples over to other markets and asset classes.

This causes a chain reaction.

In this case, a chain reaction could cause unexpected changes to market conditions that you might not have accounted for. Your algorithm might not be able to handle these changes, and thus, you run the risk of having to intervene and adjust your strategy to fit current market conditions.

These chain reactions can also happen quite rapidly, depending on how active the market exchanges are and how huge the shift in the market is. These changes can be triggered by external factors such as company mergers, the introduction of a new product, or a natural disaster.

System Failures

Given that the algorithm is held and run completely electronically, with very little human intervention, algorithmic traders do run the risk of having their hardware or software fail.

It could be that there's a power outage, or their trading computers simply aren't up to running the software anymore. In some cases, it could be that the computer systems become overloaded, which causes the power supply to blow.

No matter the cause, if something goes wrong with the hardware or software, the algorithm ceases to function, which could cause trades to halt and positions to be left open.

This can cause an increase in losses, especially if you're making high frequency or high volume trades.

In addition to the loss of trade, depending on the extent of the system failure, you might need to spend large amounts of money fixing what has been broken. This could include replacing key components, software, and in the worst-case scenario, having to build a new system altogether.

If this occurs, we recommend you access your trading account and halt all activity until you're able to get things back up and running. We also recommend that you keep backups of all your data, programs, codes, and algorithms in case of a system failure.

Having these backups will make it easier for you to get back on track once your system has been restored.

Network Connectivity

As much as your algorithm is dependent on your trading computer to function optimally, it's also dependent on having a strong internet connection. Now, if you live in a fairly advanced country or city, this shouldn't be much of a problem since WIFI has become almost commonplace in certain areas.

In addition to having access to a wireless internet connection, your connection also has to be strong and stable enough to conduct trades at a consistent rate.

If your network connection cuts out due to a power failure or nasty weather conditions, your algorithm won't be able to function correctly, and you could incur some unnecessary losses.

Unfortunately, ensuring you have a stable, reliable internet connection isn't always something you're able to control. There's always the risk that the connection might cut out and disrupt your trading.

Risk Management

We know why risk management is important, but what exactly does it entail? In simple terms, risk management is needed to reduce losses when trading or investing. Proper risk management can also be used to help protect trade and investment accounts from losing money.

As discussed above, risks occur when losses are incurred. Given the inherently risky nature of trade and investment, risk management is a necessary component of any trader's arsenal. With the proper risk management strategies in place, a trader or investor is able to access market exchanges without the fear that they'll lose all their cash (Kuepper, 2019).

While there are a few risk management strategies inherent in the process of developing a trading strategy and algorithm, having this as your only form of risk management isn't nearly enough if you want to trade successfully.

Now, depending on your trading strategy and trading methods, the risk management strategies you implement will vary. However, there are a few common risk management strategies that have universal appeal.

Here are a few **common risk management tips** that should work for the everyday trader:

Coming to Terms with Loss

This tip might sound completely out of the realm of possibility when discussing risk management. After all, the entire point of risk management is to avoid risks and losses as much as possible, right?

However, as we've mentioned previously, risks are inherent to trade. No matter how effective your strategy and how robust your risk management strategies are, there will always be some measure of risk. It is inevitable.

Because of this, we think it's really important to acknowledge the risks that come along with trade and investment and realize that each trade comes with risks. Sometimes things don't work out the way you want them to. Sometimes market trends end unexpectedly, or the market shifts in ways that you might not have predicted.

Therefore, acknowledging these risks help you better prepare for them, both emotionally and financially.

Risk management exists not to eliminate losses but to keep your losses small and manageable while ensuring that your gains outweigh your losses (Desai, 2016).

Entry Points

One of the key skills you'll need to develop in order to become a successful trader is knowing how to read the market and identify trade and investment opportunities. Part of this skill is knowing when to enter and exit positions in order to generate the best possible gains.

Knowing when to enter and exit positions is something many traders struggle with, no matter their experience level, so don't feel too discouraged if you stumble around a bit. The main problem with this aspect of trading is that there isn't a right or wrong way of doing it.

Trade and investment are generally wildly subjective, and strategies will vary from trader to trader. Therefore, it can be hard to pin down exactly how to go about trading.

However, there are a few general guidelines and pieces of advice that can help you figure things out.

If you find a rapidly growing stock or an asset that's increasing in momentum, as tempting as it might be to jump in and buy up a ton of stock, we would advise that you wait. Watch the asset carefully and wait for the asset to reach its stride. Once you've found a reliable pattern to the asset's increasing momentum, you can enter a position with the knowledge that you'll be able to spot your exit points.

In addition to this, we suggest you check out market indicators and use them as guidelines for entering and exiting positions.

Now, with algorithmic trading, knowing when to enter and exit positions shouldn't be too much of an issue since your algorithm would have been programmed with specific instructions on when to enter and exit positions.

That being said, you'll still need to decide when your

algorithm will enter and exit positions when developing your trading strategy and coding your algorithm.

Diversifying Your Portfolio

Diversifying your trading or investment portfolio is one of the most important aspects of trading. Essentially, this approach to trade is based on the age-old saying, 'Don't put all your eggs in one basket,' What this means is that, if you invest all your cash into one stock or financial instrument, you run the risk of experiencing massive losses if the stock or asset plummets.

To mitigate this risk, it's strongly advised that you diversify your portfolio by investing in and trading a wide variety of stocks and financial assets. That way, if one of them fails, the loss you'll experience won't be as devastating.

That being said, it's also important to make sure your portfolio is evenly balanced. Or at least that it's balanced according to your trading strategy. Having a properly balanced portfolio serves a similar purpose to diversifying your portfolio in that it mitigates some risk and increases the likelihood of generating profits.

See, it's really quite simple. A diversified portfolio consists of various stocks and financial assets and, therefore, affords you more opportunities to generate profits and decreases your risk of incurring major losses.

Hedging

Hedging is essentially a trading strategy that aims to offset any potential losses. This means trading and investing with the aim of reducing risks. This entails hedging against the market price risk in order to protect yourself against any negative price movements by obtaining a price lock (Thakar, 2020a).

A price lock kicks in when the price of an asset moves beyond a predetermined limit. Once this happens, all trades stop for the day or until the price moves back within the limit. For example, if the price of an asset drops below the limit, your algorithm can be programmed to halt all trading until the price moves above this limit.

This prevents you from making large losses if the price of an asset drops substantially.

This trade and investment strategy is often done using derivatives (a financial instrument) since the relationship between derivatives, and their corresponding underlying asset is clearly defined (Thakar, 2020a).

If you're not a fan of derivatives, this strategy also makes use of futures contracts, options, and over-the-counter stocks.

Implementing hedging when using algorithmic trading is pretty easy since you're able to code hard price locks, and your algorithm will abide by these price locks without much intervention.

The Risk/Reward Ratio

As mentioned, whenever a trader decides to enter or exit a trade, they need to consider the risks involved. The goal for every trader should be to have the "reward" (profit) outweigh the risks.

Therefore, if the risks associated with a trade are high and outweigh the reward, there's no point in entering it. On the other hand, if the risks associated with the trade are low and the reward outweighs the risk, it would be beneficial to enter the trade.

The risk to reward ratio trading strategy is often used by conservative traders who are more cautious when entering and exiting positions in order to lower their risk as much as possible.

While there's nothing wrong with conservative trading, we would caution against being overly cautious when trading. Allowing your fear of risk and losses to dictate your trading could cause you to miss out on generating profits. Luckily, algorithmic trading removes human emotion from the equation, so you shouldn't have much to worry about in that department.

The key challenge with the risk/reward ratio strategy is knowing how to balance the risk and the reward because, in trade and investment, the higher the risk, the higher the reward.

The risk/reward ratio you settle on will depend on the trading method you use (day risk-reward, high-frequency trading, etc.). For example, day traders should aim for a 1:2 risk/reward ratio. What this means is that if you make a $100 trade, you should be willing to lose $200.

The risk/reward ratio aims to give traders a clear idea of potential profits and losses related to each trade they make. This allows you to make informed decisions when trading. Implementing a risk/reward ratio will also prevent you from executing trades that could put your entire account at risk.

Regular Maintenance

Just like how you should regularly monitor and evaluate your algorithm, the same goes for your trading PC. For algorithmic traders, their trading PCs are their bread and butter. Without them, algorithmic trading would be impossible.

Therefore, it's vital to run regular maintenance checks on your hardware and software. Most PCs come with preinstalled tune-up programs that check the efficiency of your PC. Running tune-ups and service maintenance ensures that your PC is running in optimal condition and lowers the risk of system failures.

You could also use this time to evaluate the condition of your PC and its components and decide whether a hardware update is needed. Perhaps your power supply needs to be upgraded, or you'd like to invest in a better motherboard.

The point here is to ensure that your PC is able to keep up with your trading algorithm and run your trading ventures efficiently and effectively.

Scenario Analysis

Scenario analysis is another method that can be used to manage risks. This method involves estimating the anticipated value of a trade or investment portfolio after a predetermined period of time (Hayes, 2019). This is done on the assumption that the value of the assets held in the portfolio is subject to change, for example, a change in the interest rate.

Traders can implement scenario analysis to estimate the changes in value of their portfolios in response to hostile market changes or conditions. This method is also commonly used to estimate the value of portfolios in theoretical worst-case scenarios.

Scenario analysis is done by computing various reinvestment rates for anticipated returns that are reinvested. These calculations are based on mathematical and statistical principles (Hayes, 2019).

Using these calculations, scenario analysis provides some idea of how the value of your trading or investment portfolio might change in "what if" situations.

Essentially, it answers the question of how your trading portfolio will perform if the market crashes or if it shifts in a different direction.

Now, we know that some people insist that you should conduct a scenario analysis before you enter a trade, but in our opinion, this is a bit excessive. With an algorithm, you're able to set certain parameters and limitations. These limitations should be set with the potential risks in mind. If you've done this correctly, we think conducting scenario analysis before each and every trade is simply ridiculous.

We would advise that you implement scenario analysis at the beginning of your trading strategy development and coding so, once your algorithm is up and running, you don't have to waste time constantly doing scenario analysis since your algorithm will already be taking this into consideration.

Portfolio Optimization

Portfolio optimization involves building your portfolio with the aim of maximizing anticipated returns while minimizing the risks. Now, how you choose to optimize your portfolio will depend on your trading strategy and financial goals.

Portfolio optimization is based on the Modern Portfolio Theory (MPT). The MPT was pioneered by Harry Markowitz in his paper "Portfolio Selection," which was first published in 1952 in the Journal of Finance (Chen, 2019b). This is a theory on how traders can build portfolios to maximize anticipated returns based on the level of market risk associated with the portfolio. This theory also argues that the risk and return associated with an investment or trade shouldn't be viewed in isolation but instead should be evaluated in terms of how this investment affects the overall risk and return rates of the portfolio.

That being said, optimizing your portfolio essentially involves analyzing various portfolios that have different proportions of investments by calculating the potential risks and rewards (profits) that each portfolio could generate (Thakar, 2020a). This is done with the aim of finding the perfect combination of assets that will yield the maximum amount of profits with the least amount of risk.

Common Beginner Mistakes and How to Avoid Them

Now that we've gone over the common risks associated with algorithmic trading and how to mitigate those risks via risk management strategies, we thought it would be helpful to cover the common mistakes I've noticed among newbie traders.

Making mistakes is part of being human, and, for the most part, mistakes are inevitable. This is especially true if you're starting something new. If you're riding a bike for the first time, chances are you'll stumble and fall a few times. If you're learning how to draw, you'll probably make mistakes because you're not accustomed to the techniques and know-how that come with practice.

The same goes for trading.

If you're a newbie trader, chances are that you're going to make mistakes. However, unlike with drawing or riding a bike, you won't just walk away with a scraped knee or a poorly drawn picture. If you make a mistake in trade, you could lose money.

While mistakes are inevitable, there are a few common mistakes that beginner traders make that are easily avoidable with a bit of caution and knowledge.

Lack of Preparation

Unlike with other hobbies or interests, you can't simply create a trading account and jump into live trading without any prior knowledge or experience. The risk of major losses is high if you go ahead without doing any groundwork. While this might be okay if you're loaded, for most of us, money is tight.

Therefore, if you want to begin and succeed in trade, you'll have to have some measure of discipline. You'll have to do your research and try to learn as much about trading as you can before jumping in. In addition to that, there are a plethora of skills that you'll have to pick up before you're ready.

We've mentioned the skills you'll need to learn in Chapter 2, but let's do a quick recap. The key skills you'll need to learn include things like knowing how to read market trends, knowing how to operate online trade platforms, having a working knowledge of how trade works, such as when to exit and enter positions, when and how to trade, and which financial instruments are ideal for you and your circumstances.

In addition to forgoing the research and practice aspects of trading, we've also noticed that, when entering the world of trade, most beginners are completely unaware of how much work goes into it. With trading, there are watchlists to create and track in order to know when and where to trade. You'll need to set up charting systems to track your portfolio, not to mention trying to implement a trading strategy.

With algorithmic trading, the learning curve and requirements are even steeper (see Chapter 2).

Not knowing when and how to properly execute trades or how to do your due diligence before trading will lead to growing losses. These losses are often easily avoidable.

Now, if you're reading this book, we're assuming you're one of the few who won't make this mistake. And to help you further your pre-trade prep, we've set up the next chapter, filled with additional resources to help you on your journey.

No Planning

This mistake goes hand in hand with the one mentioned above. After all, if you're not preparing, it's very unlikely that you've entered a trade with a solid trading strategy or plan.

You might jump into live trading with the sole aim of making money fast and rush to invest in stocks or assets that you think are on the rise without much thought behind the action. However, because you rushed in without a plan, the investments and trades you made could turn against you, and you'll start to incur losses. You might even lose all that you've invested and end up in a worse position than when you started.

Another aspect of this mistake is that you could've had a trading plan or strategy in mind but, due to excitement or impatience, you strayed from that plan and made some impulsive decisions.

Having a plan and not following through could cause the same losses as if you didn't have a plan at all.

Remember, one of the key tenets of being a trader is being patient and making deliberate, informed decisions when trading. If you're impulsive, impatient, and uninformed, it is highly unlikely that you'll succeed.

Allowing Emotions to Dictate Your Trades

Another mistake that goes hand in hand with the one mentioned above is human emotion. Now, emotions aren't inherently risky, nor do they inherently cause mistakes. However, once you allow your emotions to rule your actions without thought of the consequences of those actions, that's when it becomes an issue, especially within trading.

Every trader struggles to control their emotions and gut responses when trading. It's a constant push and pull as you battle with fear, confidence, and greed.

When starting out with trade, it's likely you'll be excited and ready to jump in and begin making money. On the other hand, you could feel scared and be cautious. And both these emotions are completely normal and natural.

In most cases, these emotions are a great way of motivating you. For example, fear helps you remain cautious and prevents you from being reckless and conducting risky trades. Greed could motivate you to work harder and learn more techniques and trade methods. Confidence can help you execute trades and enter and exit positions.

However, you should be careful not to let these emotions get the best of you.

Overconfidence and greed could cause you to take huge risks with your trades, while fear could prevent you from accessing trade opportunities.

What's important is to keep a cool head and stick to your trading plan for as long as it's serving you. If you need an outlet for those impulsive emotions, we would suggest you keep a paper trading account on hand to play around with.

Difficult and Complex Trading Patterns

On the opposite side of the spectrum to the trading mistakes we've covered thus far, are traders who've done their due diligence, have done the research, and have a comfortable working knowledge of how market exchanges and trading work.

With beginners who've done the groundwork and are confident in themselves, we've often seen the mistake of them choosing very complex, difficult trading strategies to start out with.

The problem with complex trading strategies is that they are often difficult to implement and require extensive experience as well as the skill set and knowledge to pull them off. Therefore, most beginners often find their trades and strategies failing because they lack the experience to make them work effectively.

In our experience, being successful at trade requires both experience and know-how. As excited and ready as you may be, we would caution against biting off more than you can chew.

Instead, start small with simple, easy-to-implement trade strategies until you find your feet. Once you're more comfortable and have gained more experience, you can branch out and experiment with more complex strategies.

Chapter 7:
Additional Resources

This chapter lists additional resources that you can use to learn more about algorithmic trading and upgrade your coding and trading skills.

We've split this chapter into two main sections. The first section focuses on trading and algorithmic trade specifically, while the second section focuses on building a trading computer and upgrading your coding skills.

Resources for (Algorithmic) Trade and Investment

In this section, we'll be covering resources that we think are ideal for beginners when starting their trading journey. If you'd like to learn more, we'd suggest you start here.

Udemy

Udemy is a great online learning resource that offers thousands of classes covering a wide variety of topics such as trading, investment, business management, and many others.

We found it quite impressive that these courses were created in collaboration with industry professionals. We think this drastically improved the quality and reliability of the courses. In this section, we've linked a very handy trading course that we think would suit beginners.

Not only is the course professionally curated, but the information is also delivered in a beginner-friendly, simple manner which I found enjoyable.

Udemy is a paid service. However, it is quite affordable and shouldn't break the bank. Once you pay for a specific course, you'll have lifetime access to that course as well as the ability to engage with instructors if you haven't understood the lesson well.

The only possible downside is that these courses don't offer diplomas or certificates. However, we don't think this should be much of an issue since the aim is to improve your trading skills.

The Disciplined Trader

The Disciplined Trader is an excellent beginner-friendly trading book that focuses on the psychology of trading and the mental discipline one needs if one wants to be successful.

While not the most recent book (published in 1990), we found it impressive that it has stood the test of time and is still considered by many to be a must-read.

Despite tackling a quite complex topic, we thought it was very simply written and easy to read. The author has done an amazing job at describing the basic mindset and attitudes that every trader should have.

We have included the Amazon link if you're interested in checking it out.

Algorithmic Trading & DMA

Algorithmic Trading and DMA is a book written by Barry Johnson that focuses on quantitative algorithmic trading. While a bit complex, we found this book incredibly useful when trying to wrap our heads around the complex concepts within algorithmic trading and coding.

The book focuses particularly on how market exchanges work and what Johnson termed the "market microstructure."

This book is essential if you want to learn more about how to create investment and trade strategies as well as get a handle on the inner workings of financial market exchanges.

Computer and Programming Resources

Finding reliable, beginner-friendly resources regarding coding and computers can be quite difficult. Now, we'll be the first to admit that we're not the most tech-savvy group of people, nor have we ever been very good with computers. So, when searching for resources to help build our programming and computer skills, we struggled to find ones that suited our beginner status.

Everything was either too complicated or not explained well enough. That being said, here are a few beginner-friendly resources that helped us out when we started as a team.

SkillShare

Now, if you've been on the internet for a while, we're sure you must've heard of skillshare by now.

Skillshare is an online learning platform that's ridiculously affordable at only $30 per year. It's a steal!

Skillshare offers thousands of courses that cover everything from photography to programming and coding. There are also various teachers on Skillshare, so if you're not into a certain class, you can almost always find another class on something similar.

The large variety of classes allows you to choose what suits you. In addition, Skillshare also allows you to choose when and where you'd like to learn. As long as you have a strong internet connection, the world is your oyster.

In this section, we've linked the Skillshare coding classes, which we think work well for beginners. You should also be able to find classes on trade and investment.

JayzTwoCents

Now, this is somewhat unconventional, but the YouTuber, JayzTwoCents, makes excellent videos about computers, computer components, and how to build a PC. He also does a ton of reviews on computer components such as motherboards, RAM cards, and power supplies.

When we stumbled across his channel, we found his instructions and explanations quite easy to follow and extremely user-friendly. His content is also very entertaining and professionally edited, and recorded. His videos are quite personal, and it often feels like speaking to a friend.

Much like with Skillshare, YouTube allows you to watch videos whenever and wherever you want, so long as you have access to the internet. This allows you the freedom to learn whenever you wish.

In addition to this, YouTube is completely free to use. There is a Premium version; however, we find this unnecessary.

The website also offers hundreds of thousands of other YouTube channels, some of which also cover trade and investment. We suggest you hit the search bar and explore these options.

Data Camp

Data Camp is another amazing online resource that specializes in coding and programming. Much like most of the resources on this list, there is a free version and a premium paid account; however, we haven't found that this has made much of a difference in our experience.

What we found quite great is that Data Camp offers a tutorial class called *'Python For Finance: Algorithmic Trading,'* which we think you'll find quite useful when building your coding skills. After all, while learning to code is essential, you'll also need to know how to translate a trading strategy into coding and how to do it effectively.

We found that this tutorial is great for learning how to code specifically for algorithmic trading. Not only is it beginner-friendly, but it's also completely online, which means you can learn when you want and where you want.

Once again, you'll have to have an internet connection if you'd like to access this resource.

Inside the Machine: An Illustrated Introduction to Microprocessors and Computer Architecture

This is a more traditional resource. The book 'Inside the Machine' is a beginner's guide to computers and their various components.

Given that it's a beginner's guide, it's extremely user-friendly and uses simple language. We also found that it imparts information without overwhelming the reader or bombarding them with all kinds of complicated terms.

This book is aimed to help readers understand the basics of a modern computer and the different components of the computer. It also covers the basics of programming, including fundamental concepts and even some advanced lessons.

Overall, this is a great book to get you started in computers and programming, especially if you're a bit hesitant, given the technical nature of the subject.

Conclusion

And, just like that, we've reached the end of our journey together. Within the last few chapters, we've covered everything from the basics and requirements of algorithmic trading to risk management and algorithmic evaluation.

While we have tried our best to cram as much information into these chapters as humanly possible, we're afraid you've merely seen the tip of the iceberg.

As Chapter 7 demonstrated, there's a world of knowledge out there, and as you continue learning, you'll find that there is so much more that you don't know. Now, we don't mean to sound discouraging. If anything, we're hoping that our words will act as a motivator to push you onward toward greater things.

You picked up this book for a reason. It could've been simple interest, curiosity, or a desire to trade. Whatever your reason to pick it up, there is a reason you've stuck around until the very end. After all, no one forced you to finish it.

So, our question to you is, why did you stay? Curiosity only takes you so far, and we doubt it would sustain you for the length of an entire book.

If your answer is because you're truly interested in trading, then we're so glad to have had you.

As we've shown you, while trading isn't the easiest thing to pick up and master, it is possible. With the right tools at your disposal, we're sure you can reach your financial goals faster than you thought possible. All you need is patience and dedication.

As with all good things, being a master at trade and investments won't come easy. It certainly won't happen overnight. You'll have to put in the work, and it's going to be difficult, but we promise the rewards are worth it.

We can only hope that we've given you enough tools to get you started.

Now, you might be looking around wondering, what next? Where do I go from here?

Well, what happens next is entirely up to you. Your financial future is completely in your hands, and you decide where to go. You could choose to put this book away and forget all you've learned, or you could decide to pick up another finance book and equip yourself with more knowledge.

If you want to continue learning more about algorithmic trading and trade in general, Chapter 7 acts as a roadmap toward amazing resources that you can check out now that you've finished this book.

Before we see you off at the door, let us leave you with a few key takeaways, which we think sum up the lessons and information in this book pretty well. Think of it as a summary of what we've covered thus far.

Key Takeaways

In this section, we've compiled what we believe are the key tenets of the book. These are the key pieces of advice and information that we hope you'll carry with you, even if you end up forgetting everything else.

We've chosen a key tenet or takeaway from the chapters in this book to create something of a summary of lessons.

Know Your Basics

The first chapter of this book was pretty straightforward. It acted as an introduction or crash course in algorithmic trading. In many ways, it laid the foundation of what was to come.

That being said, we think that the best lesson you could learn from chapter one was to know the basics. This means being able to answer questions like *'What is algorithmic trading?'*, *'How does it work?'*, and *'What are the advantages and disadvantages of algorithmic trading?'*.

You should also be familiar with the basics of trading, trade strategies, and how they work, as well as online brokers and the role they play in financial markets.

Now, you might be asking yourself why we're so adamant for you to know these things. Well, think of it this way: when building a house, you need a strong foundation, otherwise the house might collapse.

Knowing the basics of trade and investments is your foundation. It's what your trading journey will rest on as you grow and learn. If you're unclear about the basics, you could end up making simple mistakes that could cause you to lose money and have your trading career crash down around you.

Knowing the basics is so important because it offers you a sense of familiarity and direction. It helps you make important decisions like deciding which trading strategy to go with or which broker to choose.

Be Prepared

When starting any new venture or aspiring to a new goal, it's important to know what you'll need to get to where you want to be.

Let's say that you've been wanting to get into gardening. You've done all your reading, figured out the best soil type to grow your preferred flowers in and you've even found the best location in your home to start your garden.

While that's all fine and well, you can't actually start gardening until you've acquired all the necessary tools. These could be flower pots, seeds, watering cans, and soil.

Well, the same can be said about algorithmic trading. Having the basics committed to memory is great, but that alone doesn't make you an algorithmic trader. If you want to begin trading, you'll need the right tools.

Now, with manual trading, all you'll need is a good internet connection and a trading account with a broker to begin. However, as discussed in Chapter 2, you'll need a lot more than that to begin algorithmic trading.

The point here is to be prepared when entering a new venture, especially if it's something as complex as trading.

Consistency is Key

Once you've got your trading algorithm and account up and running according to the strategy you've chosen, it's not enough to just leave it alone and hope for the best.

While algorithmic trading is a form of automated trading, it still requires human intervention. It's not something you can set up and leave running.

Instead, you'll need to consistently monitor and evaluate the performance of your algorithm in order to ensure that it remains profitable and is able to keep up with market trends.

That being said, it isn't just your algorithm that needs constant maintenance. It's important that you don't stop learning and trying to improve your skills. After all, practice makes perfect.

So, we would recommend that, even if you become comfortable with trading, you never stop researching new methods and exploring various investment and trade options. With algorithmic trading, you'll also have to keep up with your coding and programming skills.

In addition to this, due to the constantly fluctuating financial markets, it's also a good idea to maintain consistency in keeping up with financial news. This allows you to prepare for any market shifts that may occur.

Understand the Risks Involved

Let's go back to the gardening example.

Let's say you begin gardening. You've got the soil, the seeds, the right location, and a gorgeous watering can—everything you could possibly need to get started. And so, you get started with planting and sowing and everything else that goes along with gardening.

Over time, your plants sprout, and everything seems to be going well. Then, one day, you wake up to find your plants half-eaten and nearly dead. Nestled between your plants, you find little insects and snails, all of which have had a feast on your new plants.

All that hard work down the drain, and all because you forgot to become acquainted with the risks involved with gardening.

As with gardening, trading comes with its fair share of risks. Chapter 6 goes into great detail about the risks associated with algorithmic trading and how to safeguard against them.

Being aware of the risks involved with algorithmic trading is the best way to protect yourself from them.

That being said, as much as it's important to be aware of the risks involved, it is equally important to accept that risks are inherent in trade and investment.

Final Thoughts

Now that we've reached the very end of this book and we've imparted as much knowledge and advice that these pages allow, it's time for us to say goodbye.

You're on your own now, and whether you decide to pursue your interest in trading or go on as you have is completely up to you.

But we can't help but say these last words:

Do not let your time spent reading this book be in vain. Learn, explore, and put your knowledge and skills to use.

We wish you well on your trading journey.

References

6 Steps to Evaluate Your Trading Strategy for Optimal Performance. (2019). Futures Day Trading Strategies. https://optimusfutures.com/tradeblog/archives/steps-to-evaluate-trading-strategy

12 Top Tips for Monitoring Algo Trading. (2019). Eventus Systems. https://www.eventussystems.com/monitoring-algo-trading/

Algorithm Trading: Benefits and Risks. (2017). Finextra. https://www.finextra.com/blogposting/14351/algorithm-trading-benefits-amp-risks

Barone, A. (2020). Introduction to Momentum Trading. Investopedia. https://www.investopedia.com/trading/introduction-to-momentum-trading/

Bhagat, V., & Singh, A. (2018). Algorithmic Trading Strategies and Modelling Ideas. QuantInsti; QuantInsti. https://blog.quantinsti.com/algorithmic-trading-strategies/

Bloomenthal, A. (2019). What Is Arbitrage? Investopedia.

https://www.investopedia.com/ask/answers/what-is-arbitrage/

Bryant, M. R. (n.d.). Stress Testing for Trading Strategy Robustness (article): Adaptrade Software. Www.adaptrade.com. Retrieved August 4, 2021, from http://www.adaptrade.com/Newsletter/NL-StressTesting.htm

Burns, S. (2020). What is an Equity Curve? New Trader U. https://www.newtraderu.com/2020/04/12/what-is-an-equity-curve/

Chen, J. (2019a). Algorithmic Trading Definition. Investopedia. https://www.investopedia.com/terms/a/algorithmic trading.asp

Chen, J. (2019b). Modern Portfolio Theory (MPT). Investopedia. https://www.investopedia.com/terms/m/modernpo rtfoliotheory.asp

Chen, J. (2019c). Rebalancing. Investopedia. https://www.investopedia.com/terms/r/rebalancin g.asp

Chen, J. (2021). Understanding the Theory of Mean Reversion. Investopedia. https://www.investopedia.com/terms/m/meanreve rsion.asp

Davey, K. (2019). The Ultimate Guide To Successful Algorithmic Trading | Hacker Noon.

Hackernoon.com. https://hackernoon.com/the-ultimate-guide-to-successful-algo-trading-15r31fl

Desai, K. (2016). 5 Simple Tips for Risk Management for Day Traders. Bulls on Wall Street. https://bullsonwallstreet.com/risk-management-101/

Fernando, J. (2019). How to Use the Sharpe Ratio to Analyze Portfolio Risk Versus Return. Investopedia. https://www.investopedia.com/terms/s/sharperatio.asp

Fernando, J. (2021). Volume Weighted Average Price (VWAP) Definition. Investopedia. https://www.investopedia.com/terms/v/vwap.asp

Folger, J. (2019). How to Read a Strategy Performance Report. Investopedia. https://www.investopedia.com/articles/fundamental-analysis/10/strategy-performance-reports.asp

Fundamental, Technical and Sentiment Analysis. (2018). Orbex Forex Trading Blog. https://www.orbex.com/blog/en/2018/05/fundamental-technical-and-sentiment-analysis

Hayes, A. (2019). Understanding Scenario Analysis. Investopedia. https://www.investopedia.com/terms/s/scenario_analysis.asp

Hayes, A. (2020). Implementation Shortfall. Investopedia.

https://www.investopedia.com/terms/i/implementation-shortfall.asp

Johnston, M. (2021). Coding Your Own Algo-Trading Robot. Investopedia. https://www.investopedia.com/articles/active-trading/081315/how-code-your-own-algo-trading-robot.asp

Kuepper, J. (2019). Risk management techniques for active traders. Investopedia. https://www.investopedia.com/articles/trading/09/risk-management.asp

Laster, S. (n.d.). The Benefits Of Algorithmic Trading. Www.fxempire.com. Retrieved August 4, 2021, from https://www.fxempire.com/education/article/the-benefits-algorithmic-trading-397949

Louis. (2020). Best Algorithmic Trading Platforms 2021 | Trade Options With Me. Trade Options with Me. https://tradeoptionswithme.com/best-algo-trading-platforms/

Mitchell, C. (2021). How trading algorithms are created. Investopedia. https://www.investopedia.com/articles/active-trading/111214/how-trading-algorithms-are-created.asp

Percent of Volume (POV). (n.d.). Www.interactivebrokers.com. Retrieved August 16, 2021, from https://www.interactivebrokers.com/en/software/tws/usersguidebook/algos/fox_pov.htm

Planning and Executing Index Rebalance Trades | Ryedale. (2021). Www.ryedale.com. https://www.ryedale.com/insights/thought-leadership/planning-and-executing-index-rebalance-trades/

Samuelsson. (2019). Trading Computer Guide (Algo trading, Swingtrading and Daytrading). The Robust Trader. https://therobusttrader.com/trading-computer-algorithmic-swing-trading-and-daytrading/

Samuelsson. (2021). Does Algorithmic Trading Work? (With Steps to Make It Work For You!). TheRobustTrader. https://therobusttrader.com/does-algorithmic-trading-work/

Seth, S. (2021a). Basics of Algorithmic Trading: Concepts and Examples. Investopedia. https://www.investopedia.com/articles/active-trading/101014/basics-algorithmic-trading-concepts-and-examples.asp

Seth, S. (2021b). Pick the Right Algorithmic Trading Software. Investopedia. https://www.investopedia.com/articles/active-trading/090815/picking-right-algorithmic-trading-software.asp

Sharma, R. (2021). Quantitative Trading Definition. Investopedia.

https://www.investopedia.com/terms/q/quantitativ e-trading.asp

Smigel, L. (2019). Algorithmic Trading: Is It Worth It? Analyzing Alpha. https://analyzingalpha.com/algorithmic-trading-is-it-worth-it

Smith, T. (2019). Market Sentiment Definition. Investopedia. https://www.investopedia.com/terms/m/marketse ntiment.asp

Solanki, J. (2020). Automated trading vs. manual trading. Admirals. https://admiralmarkets.com/education/articles/aut omated-trading/automated-trading-vs-manual-trading

Thakar, C. (2020a). Introduction to Risk Management in Trading. QuantInsti. https://blog.quantinsti.com/trading-risk-management/

Thakar, C. (2020b). Time-Weighted Average Price (TWAP) in Financial Markets. QuantInsti. https://blog.quantinsti.com/twap/

Trading Platform - Definition, What is Trading Platform, Advantages of Trading Platform, and Latest News. (2021). Cleartax.in. https://cleartax.in/g/terms/trading-platform